Creating a
New Civilization
through Social
Entrepreneurship

Creating a New Civilization through Social Entrepreneurship

Compiled by the
Goi Peace Foundation

Patrick U. Petit, editor

With a foreword by
Muhammad Yunus

Transaction Publishers
New Brunswick (U.S.A.) and London (U.K.)

First Transaction Publication 2011
Copyright © 2009 the Goi Peace Foundation.

This book is printed on acid-free paper that meets the American National Standard for Permanence of Paper for Printed Library Materials.

Library of Congress Catalog Number: 2010030807
ISBN: 978-1-4128-1094-4
Printed in the United States of America

Library of Congress Cataloging-in-Publication Data

Petit, Patrick Uwe.
  Creating a new civilization through social entrepreneurship / Patrick U. Petit.
        p. cm.
  "Originally published in 2009 by The Goi Peace Foundation."
  Includes bibliographical references.
  ISBN 978-1-4128-1094-4 (alk. paper)
    1. Social entrepreneurship. 2. Social responsibility of business. 3. Social change. I. Title.

HD60.P44 2010
658.4'08--dc22

                                                      2010030807

Contents

PART B—SOCIAL ENTREPRENEURSHIP: RISE OF AN INNOVATIVE CITIZEN SECTOR

PART C—VALUABLE TOOLS FOR (SOCIAL) ENTREPRENEURS

Foreword

Social Business – Towards a Better Capitalism

Muhammad Yunus,
Grameen Bank, Nobel Peace Prize Laureate

I became involved in the poverty issue not as a policymaker or as a researcher. I became involved because poverty was all around me, and I could not turn away from it.

In 1974, I found it difficult to teach elegant theories of economics in the university classroom, in the backdrop of a terrible famine in Bangladesh. Suddenly, I felt the emptiness of those theories in the face of crushing hunger and poverty. I wanted to do something immediate to help people around me, even if it was just one human being, to get through another day with a little more ease. That brought me face to face with poor people's struggle to find the tiniest amounts of money to support their efforts to eke out a living. I was shocked to discover a woman in the village, borrowing less than a dollar from the money-lender, on the condition that he would have the exclusive right to buy all she produces at the price that he decides. This, to me, was a way of recruiting slave labor.

I decided to make a list of the victims of this money-lending in the village next door to our campus.

When my list was complete, it had the names of 42 victims who borrowed a total amount of US $27. I was shocked. I offered US $27 from my own pocket to get these victims out of the clutches of those money-lenders. The excitement that was created among the people by this small action got me further involved in it. If I could make so many people so happy with such a tiny amount of money, why shouldn't I do more of it?

That is what I have been trying to do ever since. The first thing I did was to try to persuade the bank located in the campus to lend money to the poor. But that did not work. They didn't agree. The bank said that the poor were not credit worthy. After all my efforts, over several months, I offered to become a guarantor for the loans to the poor. When I gave the loans, I was stunned by the result. The poor paid back their loans, on time, every time! But still I kept confronting difficulties in expanding the program through the existing banks. That was when I decided to create a separate bank for the poor. I finally succeeded in doing that in 1983. I named it Grameen Bank or Village bank.

Today, Grameen Bank gives loans to nearly 7.5 million poor people, 97 per cent of whom are women, in 80,678 villages in Bangladesh. Grameen Bank gives collateral-free income generating loans, housing loans, student loans and micro-enterprise loans to the poor families and offers a host of attractive savings, pension funds and insurance products for its members. Since it introduced them in 1984, housing loans have been used to construct 650,839 houses. The legal ownership of these houses belongs to the women themselves. We focused on women because we found giving loans to women always brought more benefits to the family.

In a cumulative way the bank has given out loans totaling about US $6.68 billion. The repayment rate is 98.02%. Grameen Bank routinely makes profit. Financially, it is self-reliant and has not taken donor money since 1995. Deposits and own resources of Grameen Bank today amount to 155 per cent of all outstanding loans. According to Grameen Bank's internal survey, 64 per cent of our borrowers have crossed the poverty line.

This idea, which began in Jobra, a small village in Bangladesh, has spread around the world and there are now Grameen type programs in almost every country.

Second Generation

It is 30 years now since we began. We keep looking at the children of our borrowers to see what has been the impact of our work on their lives. The women who are our borrowers always gave topmost priority to the children. One of the Sixteen Decisions developed and followed by them was to send children to school. Grameen Bank encouraged them, and before long all the children were going to school. Many of these children made it to the top of their class. We wanted to celebrate that, so we introduced scholarships for talented students. Many of the children went on to higher education to become doctors, engineers, college teachers and other professionals. We introduced student loans to make it easy for Grameen students to complete higher education. Now some of them have Ph.Ds.

We are creating a completely new generation that will be well equipped to take their families way out of the reach of poverty. We want to make a break in the historical continuation of poverty.

Free Market Economy

Many of the problems in the world today, including poverty, persist because of a too narrow interpretation of capitalism.

Capitalism centers around the free market. It is claimed that the freer the market, the better is the result of capitalism in solving the questions of what, how, and for whom. It is also claimed that the individual search for personal gains brings collective optimal result.

The theory of capitalism assumes that entrepreneurs are one-dimensional human beings, who are dedicated to one mission in their business lives – to maximize profit. This interpretation of capitalism insulates the entrepreneurs from all political, emotional, social, spiritual, environmental dimensions of their lives. Many of the world's problems exist because of this restriction on the players of free-market.

We have remained so impressed by the success of the free-market that we never dared to express any doubt about our basic assumption. We worked extra hard to transform ourselves, as closely as possible, into the one-dimensional human beings as conceptualized in the theory, to allow smooth functioning of free market mechanism.

I have said that capitalism is a half told story. By defining "entrepreneur" in a broader way we can change the character of capitalism radically, and solve many of the unresolved social and economic problems within the scope of the free market. Let us suppose an entrepreneur, instead of having a single source of motivation (such as, maximizing profit), now has two sources of motivation, which are mutually exclusive, but equally compelling – a) maximization of profit and b) doing good to people and the world.

Each type of motivation will lead to a separate kind of business. Let us call the first type of business a profit-maximizing business, and the second type of business a social business.

Social business will be a new kind of business introduced in the market place with the objective of making a difference to the world. Investors in the social business could get back their investment money, but will not take any dividend from the company. Profit would be ploughed back into the company to expand its outreach and improve the quality of its product or service. A social business will be a non-loss, non-dividend company.

Once social business is recognized in law, many existing companies will come forward to create social businesses in addition to their foundation activities. Many activists from the non-profit sector will also find this an attractive option. Unlike the non-profit sector where one needs to collect donations to keep activities going, a social business will be self-sustaining and create surplus for expansion since it is a non-loss enterprise. Social business will go into a new type of capital market of its own, to raise capital.

Young people all around the world, particularly in rich countries, will find the concept of social business very appealing since it will give them a challenge to make a difference by using their creative talent.

Almost all social and economic problems of the world will be addressed through social businesses. The challenge is to innovate business models and apply them to produce desired social results cost-effectively and efficiently such as healthcare for the poor could be a social business, financial services for the poor, information technology for the poor, education and training for the poor, marketing for the poor, renewable energy – these are all exciting ideas for social businesses.

Social business is important because it addresses very vital concerns of mankind. It can change the lives of the bottom 60 per cent of world population and help them to get out of poverty.

We cannot cope with the problem of poverty within the orthodoxy of capitalism preached and practised today. With the failure of many Third World governments in running businesses, health, education, and welfare programmes efficiently everyone is quick to recommend – "hand it over to the private sector." I endorse this recommendation whole-heartedly. But I raise a question with it. Which private sector are we talking about? Personal profit based private sector has its own clear agenda. It comes in serious conflict with the pro-poor, pro-women, pro-environment agenda. Economic theory has not provided us with any alternative to this familiar private sector. I argue that we can create a powerful alternative – a social-consciousness-driven private sector, created by social entrepreneurs.

Grameen´s Social Business

Even profit maximizing companies can be designed as social businesses by giving full or majority ownership to the poor. This constitutes a second type of social business. Grameen Bank falls under this category of social business. It is owned by the poor.

The poor could get the shares of these companies as gifts by donors, or they could buy the shares with their own money. The borrowers buy Grameen Bank shares with their own money, and these shares cannot be transferred to non-borrowers. A committed professional team does the day-to-day running of the bank.

Bilateral and multi-lateral donors could easily create this type of social business. When a donor gives a loan or a grant to build a bridge in the recipient country, it could create instead a "bridge company" owned by the local poor. A committed management company could be given the responsibility of running the company. Profit of the company will go to the local poor as dividend, and towards building more bridges. Many infrastructure projects, like roads, highways, airports, seaports, utility companies could all be built in this manner.

Grameen has created two social businesses of the first type. One is a yogurt factory, to produce fortified yogurt to bring nutrition to malnourished children. It is a joint venture with Danone. It will continue to expand until all malnourished children of Bangladesh are reached with fortified yogurt. Another is a chain of eye-care hospitals. Each hospital will undertake, on an average, 10,000 cataract surgeries per year at differentiated prices to the rich and the poor.

Social Stock Market

To connect investors with social businesses, we need to create social stock market where only the shares of social businesses will be traded. An investor will come to this stock-exchange with a clear intention of finding a social business, which has a mission of his or her liking. Anyone who wants to make money will go to the existing stock-market.

To enable a social stock-exchange to perform properly, we will need to create rating agencies, standardization of terminology, definitions, impact measurement tools, reporting formats, and new financial publications, such as, *The Social Wall Street Journal*. Business schools will offer courses and business management degrees on social businesses to train young managers how to manage social business enterprises in the most efficient manner, and, most of all, to inspire them to become social business entrepreneurs themselves.

Role Of Businesses In Globalization

I support globalization and believe it can bring more benefits to the poor. But it must be the right kind of globalization. To me, globalization is like a hundred-lane highway criss-crossing the world. If it is a free-for-all highway, its lanes will be taken over by the giant trucks from powerful economies. Bangladeshi rickshaws will be thrown off the highway. In order to have a win-win globalization we must have traffic rules, traffic police, and traffic authority for this global highway. Rule of "strongest takes it all" must be replaced by rules that ensure that the poorest have a place and piece of the action, without being elbowed out by the strong. Globalization must not become financial imperialism.

Powerful multi-national social businesses can be created to retain the benefit of globalization for the poor people and poor countries. Social businesses will either bring ownership to the poor people, or keep the profit within the poor countries, since taking dividends will not be their objective. Direct foreign investment by foreign social businesses will be exciting news for recipient countries. Building strong economies in the poor countries by protecting their national interest from plundering companies will be a major area of interest for the social businesses.

We Can Put Poverty In The Museums

I believe that we can create a poverty-free world because poverty is not created by poor people. It has been created and sustained by the economic and social system that we have designed for ourselves; the institutions and concepts that make up that system; the policies that we pursue.

Poverty is created because we built our theoretical framework on assumptions which under-estimates human capacity, by designing concepts, which are too narrow (such as concept of business, concept of credit-worthiness, concept of entrepreneurship, concept of employment) or developing institutions, which remain half-done (such as financial institutions, where poor are left out). Poverty is caused by the failure at the conceptual level, rather than any lack of capability on the part of people.

I firmly believe that we can create a poverty-free world if we collectively believe in it. In a poverty-free world, the only place you would be able to see poverty is in the poverty museums. When school children take a tour of the poverty museums, they would be horrified to see the misery and indignity that some human beings had to go through. They would blame their forefathers for tolerating this inhuman condition, which existed for so long, for so many people.

A human being is born into this world fully equipped not only to take care of himself or herself, but also to contribute to enlarging the well being of the world as a whole. Some get the chance to explore their potential to some degree, but many others never get any opportunity, during their lifetime, to unwrap the wonderful gift they were born with. They die unexplored and the world remains deprived of their capacity, and their contribution.

Grameen has given me an unshakeable faith in the creativity of human beings. This has led me to believe that human beings are not born to suffer the misery of hunger and poverty.

To me poor people are like bonsai trees. When you plant the best seed of the tallest tree in a flower-pot, you get a replica of the tallest tree, only inches tall. There is nothing wrong with the seed you planted, only the soil-base that is given to it is too inadequate. Poor people are bonsai people. There is nothing wrong in their seeds. Simply, society never gave them the base to grow on. All it needs to get the poor people out of poverty for us to create an enabling environment for them. Once the poor can unleash his or her energy and creativity, poverty will disappear very quickly.

Let us join hands to give every human being a fair chance to unleash his or her energy and creativity.

Preface

Patrick U. Petit, Editor

Humanity is confronted with the gravest financial crisis and economic recession since the Great Depression. Political leaders, national ministries of finance and central banks around the world are trying to prop up their country's sinking economy and arrest a downward economic spiral by innovating financial rescue and bank bailout plans, as well as economic stimulus and recovery packages.

All these measures are being taken to reestablish trust in the economy and to trigger an economic revival. Despite these efforts, however, stagnation seems everlasting as uncertainty leads to collective fear, which puts spending and investing decisions by businesses and consumers on hold.

Collective fear and panic can sink humanity into another Great Depression. The latter was a worldwide economic downturn originated in the United States in 1929, when the stock market crashed and became a worldwide business slump throughout the 1930's affecting almost all countries. It was the largest and most significant economic depression in modern history. During that period, US President Franklin D. Roosevelt launched the New Deal, a sequence of governmental initiatives and social programs aimed to recover the economy, reform business and financial practices and create jobs. The New Deal had the objective to mitigate the effects of the Great Depression, and most importantly, to restore a sense of confidence to the people.

Today's economic crisis has spread joblessness and distress across the world and has opened many people's eyes to growing social inequalities. Resolving this crisis will require both boldness and creativity. There is an increasing sense of urgency that a new wave of innovation, creativity and entrepreneurial solutions are needed to meet the challenges of defeating inequalities, improving environmental stewardship, and boosting social and economical development for all people on the planet.

In the past decade, social entrepreneurship has come to the forefront of global development. Social entrepreneurs play a vital role in fostering societal change. Using entrepreneurial principles, they establish new ventures to improve the lives of millions of people by implementing system changes in education, environment, health, human rights, social equity and integration, economic development and other areas. One well-known contemporary social entrepreneur is Muhammad Yunus, 2006 Nobel Peace Prize winner and founder of the Grameen Bank, whose genuine motives behind his success is illustrated in the foreword of this book.

The global grassroots movement of social entrepreneurs is attracting growing amounts of attention, talent and money, and has become a major force in driving innovation to solve society's most pressing social problems. Today, social entrepreneurs are working in more than one hundred countries to create opportunity for people who otherwise would stay in poverty and continue facing deprivation. They and their fields of work are as varied as the communities they aim to serve.

While the New Deal in the 1930's was elaborated and implemented by government to mitigate the economic crisis, social entrepreneurship can be regarded as a People's New Deal, originating from the citizen sector. This People's New Deal is a powerful initiative of the 21st century to complement governmental economic stimulus and recovery packages.

Social entrepreneurs are essential to the restoration of a sustainable planet and the improvement of lives of billions of people, especially of those living in extreme poverty.

Therefore, social entrepreneurs deserve further recognition and support by the international community – by governments, multinational companies and philanthropic organizations. Furthermore, the establishment of a strong global partnership between governments, social entrepreneurs and the private sector at the national and international levels would be of great benefit to humanity.

We would like to extend our heartfelt gratitude to the distinguished authors and organizations, which have contributed to this book on social entrepreneurship. Their innovative initiatives and creative activities are inspiring examples for us to follow as we seek to achieve a harmonious and peaceful world with social equity and economic prosperity for all. As the father of social entrepreneurship Bill Drayton advocates, we are headed for a world where "Everyone is a Changemaker."

Munich, Summer 2009

Introduction

Hiroo Saionji, The Goi Peace Foundation

The Goi Peace Foundation is pleased to present this publication as a part of its Initiative for Creating a New Civilization.

The Creating a New Civilization Initiative, which our foundation launched together with our partners in 2005, brings together organizations and individuals who see the pressing need to respond to the environmental, social and economic crises confronting us today. Our aim is to network various innovative activities and people creating positive impact on the world, and build a critical mass of humans that could facilitate the transformation of our cultures and co-create a sustainable and harmonious planetary civilization based on reverence for all life, respect for our diversity, gratitude for nature, and emphasis on spiritual values.

As a way to synthesize fresh approaches toward creating a new civilization, the Goi Peace Foundation proposes the "4-S Concept" – an integrated platform with four foundational pillars: Sustainability, Systems, Science and Spirituality.

The first "S" – Sustainability – concerns the survival of the Earth itself, with its nature and ecological systems. Environmental, social and economic problems – such as global warming, resource depletion, wealth disparity and cross-cultural conflicts – are all interconnected global issues caused by human activities that are threatening our very survival. We are at a bifurcation point where we either continue on the present path toward destruction or choose the path to a sustainable future.

The second "S" – Systems – refers to the various systems we human beings have established, including our economic and political systems. Humanity is a part of the larger natural living systems of Earth. How can we harmonize our human systems with the principles of nature and the ecosystems? Our current institutions and various sociocultural systems are unsustainable and need to be transformed to operate as a whole system on a planetary scale.

The third "S" – Science – is an important component in creating a new civilization. At the cutting edge of the sciences – including physics, cosmology, the life sciences, and consciousness research – new worldviews are emerging together with a deeper understanding of life. These new sciences could bring about a paradigm shift that could be the key inspiration and foundation for building a new civilization.

The forth and final "S" – Spirituality – includes personal experience, but also has a more universal implication. The inner awakening and the empowered creativity of individuals are the real forces that will shape our collective future. Our behaviors and priorities will drastically change if we evolve our consciousness to a higher level and experience the interconnectedness of all life. We must ensure that all human activities in our future global society, whether politics, economics or business, are founded on spiritual values.

These four components are obviously interdependent. Our immediate task is to transform our systems in order to move beyond the imminent crises and ensure sustainability of our planet. At the same time, we must broaden our perspective to see the larger story of who we are and where the next stage of human evolution will lead us.

In 2008, the Goi Peace Foundation published a book entitled *Earthrise: The Dawning of a New Civilization in the 21st Century*, highlighting pioneer organizations in diverse fields that are paving the path for the emerging new civilization.

To further the initiative, we present our latest publications under the following titles:

Earth Capitalism–Creating a New Civilization through a Responsible Market Economy

Creating a New Civilization through Social Entrepreneurship

These volumes offer some concrete strategies and practices for creating a new civilization. They come out at a particularly appropriate time, when the current global financial and economic crises are causing widespread anxiety, and at the same time affirming our conviction that this is the unprecedented opportunity for change.

Earth Capitalism compiles articles by forward-thinking scientists, economists, business leaders and social activists with strategic visions for a more just and sustainable world. It introduces concepts for a new economic paradigm supported by concrete ideas for alternative models of economy and innovative ways in which future business may be conducted.

Creating a New Civilization through Social Entrepreneurship highlights the global movement of social entrepreneurship and some of the leading organizations that are advancing this citizen sector movement. While looking at this social trend in the context of a larger global transition we are currently going through, the volume also presents examples of innovative individuals that are tackling major social problems and triggering systemic change.

The core message repeated throughout both books is that in order to solve the complex global problems of today, it is not enough to simply patch up the existing civilization founded on an old paradigm. If we are to construct a better and promising future for all, we need to change our thinking and acting, adopting new values, priorities and deep wisdom.

Throughout the past century, we human beings mostly valued material things, and strove to create materially affluent lives for ourselves. We focused our efforts and energy into development and production, promoting lifestyles governed by speed, greed, and consumerism. While this materially oriented preoccupation fostered a great expansion of material civilization, we now know we can no longer continue on this way. We must shift our focus on the outer and material world to the development of our inner spiritual world. It is time we stop and rethink what is truly valuable and what real happiness is for humanity.

The articles you will read in these two volumes tell us that there are a growing number of people around the world who have awakened to altruistic values and planetary consciousness and are actively carrying out their mission as a responsible member of the global community. As social entrepreneurs and business leaders, they are optimizing their innovative minds and creative power to serve society, giving new meaning to capitalism and democracy.

We hope that the reading will ignite the love, courage and compassion and the entrepreneurial spirit in you, so that you may play your unique role in creating a new civilization. Now more than ever, each one of us is called upon to become an agent for positive change.

Tokyo, Summer 2009

Part A

The Future of Entrepreneurship
from a Global and Holistic Perspective

What Will Happen in Capitalist Societies in the Future?

– A Dialogue on the Future of Modern Civilization –

Hiroshi Tasaka, The Japan Social Entrepreneur Forum

Human Society is Developing Dialectically

*What will happen in capitalist societies in the future?

This question is an extremely important one today at a moment when global capitalism is being confronted by some extremely serious obstacles. But because the question is historical in its dimensions, simply relying on a "technology to predict the future" will not provide the answers. What we need, instead, is to understand a "philosophy to foresee the future." In other words, we need to understand a philosophy that talks about the laws that underlie change, development, and evolution in our world.

*What kind of philosophy is the philosophy to foresee the future?

Dialectic. In Western philosophy, dialectic began in Greece with Socrates and was systematized by Georg Hegel, the German Idealist philosopher. Also, Karl Marx used this philosophy in his theory of social change and Jean-Paul Sartre discussed its tenets in the context of Existentialism. In Eastern philosophy as well, dialectic has been dealt with at a profound level by Buddhist, Taoist, Esoteric Buddhist, Zen and other thinkers. Dialectic offers two laws in particular that are extremely helpful when foreseeing the future of capitalist societies: the "law of development through spiral process" and the "law of development through interpenetration of opposing objects."

*What is the law of development through spiral process?

This is the law which says that the world develops as if it were climbing a spiral staircase. In other words, if you look from the side at people ascending a spiral staircase, they appear to be progressing and developing because they are heading upward. However, if you look at them from above, they complete one revolution and return to their original positions. Therefore it appears that the revival and restoration of old things occur. But on a spiral staircase, people do not merely return to their original positions; they always move to a higher level. Similarly, in "spiral development," there is not simply revival and restoration. Rather, something develops to a new stage and this enables old things to add new value as they are revived and restored.

*What are specific examples of the law of development through spiral process?

For example, two leading-edge business models which have emerged from the Internet revolution: the "Net auction" and the "reverse auction." These models are, in fact, revivals of old nostalgic business models. Previously, before the development of capitalism, trading methods such as "bidding" and "limit pricing" existed in every market. Having once been eclipsed by the development of capitalism demanding rationalization, they have gained new life as a result of the Net revolution. But there is a difference: while one could bid or limit prices with only several hundreds of people in the past, the Net auctions and reverse auctions can involve millions of participants. These methods have indeed revived at a higher level of the spiral staircase. Likewise, e-mail represents a revival of the nostalgic culture of "letter writing" within the context of a new system. And e-learning is certainly the revival of "private tutoring" and other forms of individualized learning in a more advanced and sophisticated form.

*What then is the law of development through interpenetration of opposing objects?

It is the law which says that things which oppose and compete with each other come to resemble each other through interpenetration. For example, the policies of opposing political parties, such as those of the Conservative and Labor Parties in the UK, end up becoming alike. The way in which capitalism and socialism have learned from each other's policies, adopting approaches to social welfare on the one hand and the principles of market competition on the other, is another case in point.

The Voluntary Economy Will Revive Through Spiral Development

*Then, based on these two laws of dialectic, what will happen in capitalist societies in the future?

Capitalism will evolve into an entirely different form of capitalism in the future. This is because such spiral development and interpenetration will occur in the "economic principles" on which capitalism has traditionally been premised.

*Specifically, what affect will the law of spiral development have on these economic principles?

In capitalist societies today, the economic principle that so clearly predominates is the "monetary economy." However, the oldest economic principle in human society, the "voluntary economy," will revive and begin to have a major impact on society.

*What kind of economic principle is the voluntary economy?

The capitalism of today is premised on an economic principle called the monetary economy. The monetary economy is an economic activity in which people act with the aim of "acquiring money." By contrast, the voluntary economy is an economic activity in which people act with the aim not of "acquiring money" but of "satisfying mind." In other words, in a voluntary economy people cooperate out of goodwill and kindness, share their knowledge and wisdom, and work together in a spontaneous way.

*Is the voluntary economy an old economic principle?

Yes. The voluntary economy is actually the oldest economic principle in human history. This is because before "money" was invented and the monetary economy came into being, humankind carried out its economic activity in the "barter economy" (the exchange economy), in which things were exchanged directly for other things. But in the primitive communities that existed before barter arose, the "gift economy" prevailed, in which people gave things of value to other people out of goodwill and kindness. In such communities, in other words, the voluntary economy was front and center.

*Did the voluntary economy disappear because of the development of society?

No, that is not what happened. The "voluntary economy" has consistently remained an important economic principle throughout human history. It is because that even today certain kinds of economic activity, such as housework, child care, education in the home, caring for the elderly, community service, and so on, are occurring without an exchange of money in every corner of society, based on goodwill and kindness and on friendship and affection among people. Therefore, if the voluntary economy ceased to exist, the monetary economy would also, at that very moment, be forced to halt its activities. Let us say, for example, that families no longer provided any education to children on matters of discipline or manners. In this case, with only school education to rely on, society would no longer produce any talented people capable of working cooperatively.

The Internet Revolution will Accelerate Spiral Development and Interpenetration of Opposing Objects in the Economy

*Despite such obvious importance, why has the voluntary economy not been valued very highly until now?

There are two reasons why the voluntary economy was relegated to the position of a "shadow economy" in the long course of human history. The first is that its activities were limited to the "narrow domains" of the household or the community. The second is that the true picture of this economy remained "invisible" because it could not be evaluated in terms of the objective measure of "money."

*If that is so, why will this voluntary economy now revive and begin increasing its impact in coming society?

It is because the Internet revolution has occurred. As a result of this revolution, conditions have changed. Firstly, the Net revolution has liberated the voluntary economy from the bonds of these "narrow domains." In the Internet community today, people from around the world can gather, share their knowledge and wisdom, and cooperate with one another. Their activities can then have a global impact through the Internet. Secondly, the Net revolution has made the voluntary economy "visible." Although its activities still cannot be evaluated quantitatively in terms of "money," these activities can now be seen by large numbers of people through the "Net." The Linux Community, in which engineers from around the world gather without compensation and continue to develop and improve this operating system, is a representative case.

A Hybrid Economy will Emerge through Inter-penetration of Opposing Objects

*As the voluntary economy continues to exert a greater impact, what else will occur as a result?

The second law of dialectic will come into play, which is the "law of development through interpenetration of opposing objects." Consequently, economic principles will take a major evolutionary step forward.

*What affect will the law of interpenetration of opposing objects have on economic principles?

The two principles that now stand in opposition, the monetary economy and the voluntary economy, will begin to interpenetrate and merge. This will give rise to a "new economic principle" which we should call the "hybrid economy."

*Is this a theoretical forecast based on dialectic?

No, this principle is already a reality. Take, for example, Amazon. com, the Internet bookseller. In the context of the monetary economy, Amazon.com has created an extremely profitable business model. But, the most popular service on its site is the grassroots reviews, which owes its existence to the voluntary economy. In other words, Amazon. com's business model arises out of a hybrid economy and is not merely a "business model" but rather something that should be called a new "social system." Another example is the rapidly expanding method of "prosumer-based product development." In this method, "companies that make products" (producers) gather in the Net community with "people who use them" (consumers); both sides share knowledge and wisdom, and cooperate in the task of developing new products and services. This business model, too, is supported by the voluntary activity of consumers. It should thus also be referred to as a social system that has emerged from a hybrid economy.

*Do these activities occur only in the world of the Internet?

No, these kinds of activities also occur frequently in the real world. But there is one major reason why so many examples of spiral development and interpenetration of dialectical laws can be found in the Internet world. This is because, as indicated by the terms "dog year" and "mouse year," the changes to things in this world are accelerating; and what once took place over a period of seven or eighteen years now happens in a single year. As a result, whereas we human beings once ascended the spiral staircase leisurely over several hundred years, we are "running up" the stairs in several decades. That is why today the theme of the dialectical development of society, which was once the purview of historians and philosophers, is now an everyday concern for politicians, administrators and managers.

*What then are some examples of the hybrid economy occurring in the real world?

In fact, the most emblematic examples of the hybrid economy are the trends toward "corporate social responsibility" (CSR) and "social entrepreneurship."

Alliance between Companies and Social Entrepreneurs will Prompt an Evolution of Capitalism

*Why does CSR reflect a movement toward a hybrid economy?

The CSR movement has become a major global trend, as evidenced by the ISO's formulation of international standards with respect to CSR. And, in recent years, this movement has extended beyond the narrow scope of simply compliance or corporate ethics and has moved toward a more broadly encompassing approach of how to contribute to society as a company. These movements by companies whose essential aim is to earn "business profits" represent an increasing recognition of the value of "social contributions," and can be seen, so to speak, as interpenetration from the monetary economy toward the voluntary economy.

*Why does social entrepreneurship reflect a movement toward a hybrid economy?

On the other hand, social entrepreneurship has also become a major global trend. Social entrepreneurship arose in response to the increasingly severe difficulties that traditional non-profit organizations are having in sustaining their undertakings as government supports and benefactors contribution are discontinued. To overcome these problems, social entrepreneurs attempt to generate profits from their own undertakings and to use these profits to achieve organizational independence and sustainability. These movements by organizations whose essential aim is "social contributions" represent an increasing recognition of the value of "business profits," and can be seen, so to speak, as interpenetration from the voluntary economy toward the monetary economy.

*What will be the movements of CSR and social entrepreneurship from now?

Based on the law of interpenetration of dialectic, the movements of CSR and social entrepreneurship will inevitably converge over the long term. In other words, what have traditionally been referred to as "for-profit companies" and "non-profit organizations" will evolve and interpenetrate each other, resulting in all companies and organizations eventually becoming what are called "social enterprises." To put it another way, whether the organization is a large corporation or a small venture start-up, a NPO or a social venture, the age will come when all organizations whatever their form will be compelled to respond simultaneously to two challenges, posed in the following two questions. The first question is "Through businesses, what is the organization doing to contribute to society or to bring about social change?" The second question is "How will the organization earn profits from its undertakings in order to sustain the organization's undertakings?" In a fundamental sense, all companies and organizations will have to succeed in establishing the viability of both social contributions and business profits.

*Specifically, what should be done to promote a paradigm shift towards the hybrid economy and to encourage many companies to evolve into social enterprises?

We can do this by pursuing a "social alliance," which can be described as a situation where for-profit companies and social entrepreneurs ally each other and seek to evolve into social enterprises through an exchange of knowledge and wisdom and mutual learning. This kind of alliance differs from the ordinary "business alliances" in that both parties aim to co-evolve into a social enterprise. Specifically, it is considered that for-profit companies would provide social entrepreneurs with brands, marketing channels, and business know-how, while social entrepreneurs would provide for-profit companies with grassroots consumer networks, grassroots consumers' voice, know-how about operating voluntary communities, and other input. Already, a coffee-shop-chain company is providing access to its network of stores to a social entrepreneur who is engaged in efforts to establish fair trade in the coffee business. In return, the social entrepreneur is providing the company with an opportunity to contribute to society. In the coming age, companies are likely to pursue "social alliances" as one vital aspect of their CSR.

*What kind of enterprises will such social enterprises evolve into?

They will evolve into "earth enterprises." In this era of the global environmental problems, social enterprises that recognize their responsibilities toward "society" and seek to contribute to society will invariably become aware of their responsibilities toward "the Earth" as a whole, and then aim to become companies that contribute to the sustainability of the living system that is the Earth. The hybrid economy in which these "earth enterprises" are rooted will, in fact, go on to play an extremely important role in solving the global environmental problems.

*In what way will the hybrid economy play an important role in solving the global environmental problems?

Until now, a method from economics known as the "internalization of external cost" has primarily been relied on to solve the environmental problems. This is a method to bring "external costs," which arise outside the market economy, such as the damage caused by environmental destruction, into the market through environmental regulation and have them reflected in company costs. This can be considered a method to pay for the cost of environmental destruction by bringing these costs within the monetary economy. Emissions trading which deals with the problem of global warming is a concrete example of this approach. In addition, however, to solve the global environmental problems, the methods that link the monetary economy and the voluntary economy, that is, methods that utilize the hybrid economy will become extremely important hereafter.

*Specifically, what are some of these methods?

For example, there are "carbon offset products." These can be described as follows: When a company sells a certain product, it promises to use a part of the selling price of the product to capture the identical amount of CO_2 that is emitted during the manufacturing of that product. These carbon offset products tie the "business models" of companies to the "voluntary minds" of consumers and can be considered a new system of the hybrid economy. On the other hand, the use of what is called "corporate currency," which includes such things as airline mileage and credit card membership rewards programs, is expanding today. A system in which consumers donate this corporate currency to NPOs or social entrepreneurs of their choice has emerged. This, too, can be considered a new system of the hybrid economy.

A Paradigm Shift toward Participatory Innovation will Occur

*Then, when a paradigm shift in "economic principles" occurs, what will happen next in capitalist societies?**

A paradigm shift in "innovation" will occur. That is to say, we see a paradigm shift from traditional "beneficiary innovation" toward "participatory innovation."

*What kind of innovation is "participatory innovation?"**

Until now, in capitalist societies, something called "beneficiary innovation" has prevailed. In this innovation, a small number of exceptionally talented experts drive innovation in technologies and products, in services and businesses, and in systems and institutions, while a large number of people are placed in the position of merely receiving the benefits of such innovation. However, in societies in the near future, a large number of people will begin participating directly in the process of innovation. Examples of such participation include prosumer-based product development and open-source policy making. These are illustrations of what we might call "participatory innovation."

*What does the paradigm shift toward participatory innovation mean for social entrepreneurs?**

The role of social entrepreneurs is to drive "social innovation." When social innovation and participatory innovation become linked together, social innovation becomes an even larger and more powerful trend.

Direct Democracy will also Revive in the Fields of Economy and Culture

*When this kind of paradigm shift in "innovation" occurs, what will happen next in capitalist societies?**

A major paradigm shift will occur in "democracy." It is because direct democracy expands not only in the domain of politics but also in the domains of economy and culture.

*What does "direct democracy in economy and culture" mean?

Firstly, as a result of the Internet revolution, a large number of people are finding it easy to express their own opinions and ideas. So, rather than traditional "indirect democracy," where people choose decision makers and delegate their decision making to them, this revolution has facilitated the establishment of "direct democracy," where people participate directly in decision making. Therefore, a paradigm shift to "direct democracy" will occur in various fields from now. This kind of direct democracy will then become a reality not only in the domain of politics but also in the domains of economy and culture. Traditionally, it was generally thought that democracy was a political problem. In fact, however, it has been an economic and cultural problem as well. And, the traditional economy and culture have long been placed in a condition of indirect democracy.

*What constitutes direct democracy in the domain of economy?

In the world of economy, although a large number of consumers had different and diverse needs, companies comprehended these needs through the broad-brush approach of the "market research." Almost as if, as a consequence, they had adopted the "representative system," companies have developed products to meet the largest common denominator and supplied these products to the market. However, in the coming age, because of the expanding use of the following three methods, prosumer-based development, Long Tail marketing, and high-mix low-volume production, consumers will say what they truly want in a product and actually be able to obtain these products. In other words, direct democracy in product development will become a reality. Similarly, today rapidly expanding "affiliate programs," in which consumers recommend products that they like and encourage others to purchase them on their personal websites and blogs, can be viewed, in one sense, as the realization of direct democracy in marketing.

*What then constitutes direct democracy in the domain of culture?

Until now, in capitalist societies, as in economy, culture has also been created through the representative system and indirect democracy. For example, in the world of music, artists have been discovered by a few major labels or large production companies, which then have engineered booms and have created musical culture. However, in the coming age, a large number of people will easily be able to compose and perform their own music and release it to the rest of the world over the Internet. They will also be able freely to review and recommend the music of their favorite artists. For a large number of people, this will signify the realization of direct democracy in the creation of culture and the beginning of "an era in which culture is personally created" instead of "an era in which culture is unilaterally provided."

*Then, why is direct democracy in economy and culture important?

It is because it will change people's consciousness of democracy. Until now, democracy has been understood as participation in the "decision making" process of society. However, through the realization of direct democracy in economy and culture, the consciousness of a large number of people will begin to change. In other words, the meaning of democracy for many people will change. It will come to mean not merely participation in "decision making" but participation in "social innovation."

Knowledge Capitalism will Deepen into EMPA-thy Capitalism

*When a paradigm shift in "democracy" occurs, what will happen next in capitalist societies?

The paradigm of "knowledge capitalism" will change. "Knowledge capitalism" can be defined as capitalism in which the most important management resource is knowledge capital. In the society of the future, however, as participatory innovation takes center stage and direct democracy in economy and culture spreads, the meaning of the term "knowledge capital" will fundamentally change.

*Why will the meaning of knowledge capital change?

It is because we will enter an age of "collective intelligence." In other words, in the era of participatory innovation and direct democracy in economy and culture, it will become crucial to utilize the wisdom of many people at the grassroots as well as the knowledge of a small number of experts. In the context of the Internet revolution, this wisdom is referred to as "collective intelligence" or "wisdom of crowds." Companies in the coming age will be required to utilize such collective intelligence as knowledge capital.

*Then, what is important for utilizing collective intelligence?

One might venture to call it "empathy capital." In other words, the degree to which those companies obtain empathy from consumers becomes extremely important. This is because collective intelligence is not a management resource in the monetary economy which can be merchandised with "monetary capital"; rather, it is a management resource in the voluntary economy. To put it differently, collective intelligence is a management resource that can be exchanged for something that we should call "empathy capital," which includes empathy, trust and a good reputation from the consumer. And, for companies in the coming age, "empathy capital" will become especially important. Therefore, today's knowledge capitalism will deepen into something that we should call "empathy capitalism."

*What then should companies do to obtain "empathy capital?"

Above all, companies must evolve into "social enterprises" which highly value their contributions to society. They must then also evolve into "earth enterprises."

Capitalist Societies will Evolve into Living Systems

*Then, what kind of societies will emerge when capitalist societies become characterized by terms such as the Internet revolution, the hybrid economy, participatory innovation, direct democracy in economy and culture, empathy capitalism, and the like?

The capitalist societies of the future will become an extremely sophisticated and advanced living system," in which "living phenomena" frequently occur. Such phenomena include self-organization and emergence, evolution and co-evolution, the formation of ecosystems and the butterfly effect, and so forth.

*Then, why will capitalist societies evolve into "living systems?"

It is because companies, markets and societies will increasingly take on the properties of "complex systems." In other words, the Internet revolution, the hybrid economy, participatory innovation, direct democracy in economy and culture, and empathy capitalism all enhance the inter-relationship of people within companies, markets and societies, causing them to heighten the "complexity" of such systems. The cultural anthropologist Gregory Bateson once said that "In complex things, life dwells." As Bateson pointed out, as the complexity of systems increases, they do indeed begin to display behaviors of living systems.

*Why will the terms which characterize the future capitalist societies mentioned above enhance the inter-relationship of people in companies, markets and societies?

There are three reasons for this. Firstly, the Internet revolution will amplify the informational connections among people in companies, markets and societies. Secondly, the hybrid economy and empathy capitalism will connect people closely together not only through financial relationships but also through relationships based on goodwill, kindness, empathy, and trust. Thirdly, participatory innovation and direct democracy will increase people's motivation to connect with each other.

*What will happen when capitalist societies increasingly take on the properties of living systems?

Of particular importance in this regard is the "butterfly effect." As expressed meta-phorically, "when a butterfly flutters its wings in Beijing, it sets off a hurricane in New York," meaning that a slight fluctuation in a small part of a system will cause large changes in the system as a whole. This can sometimes appear in negative forms, such as when the economic failure of one industry in one country sparks a worldwide recession. On the other hand, it is also possible that a single social entrepreneur or a single social enterprise can change the direction of the world in a positive way. In other words, social entrepreneurs and social enterprises will be able to use the "evolution of capitalism" as a tailwind and "wisdom to cope with living systems" as a rudder in changing society in the coming age.

*Then, where can the wisdom to deal with capitalist societies as living systems be found?

Unfortunately, much of this kind of wisdom cannot be found inside modern civilization, which has developed on the basis of the mechanical system paradigm. Such wisdom, in fact, exists in the "old civilizations" which are found in each country. The reason is that, without exception, old civilizations in each country formed the foundation to the kind of wisdom that emerged from the living system paradigm. Such wisdom includes knowing how to live in harmony with the environment, how to create empathy in society, and how to temper the insatiable desires of the human beings. Consequently, in the process of evolution, capitalist societies of the future will incorporate the wisdom which resides in old civilizations and give birth to a "new civilization." That evolution is also a process of spiral development and interpenetration, that is, exactly the dialectical development of human civilization.

Entrepreneurship for a Better World

Peter Spiegel, GENISIS Institute

A paradigm shift is about to happen. For the first twenty years following the advent of the environmental movement, economics and ecology were seen as opposites, even as inimical to each other. It was not until the mid-1990s that more and more people realised that economics and ecology are ideally complementary; when linked together in an intelligent way, they can become a mutually-propelling turbo engine.

Today we are about to experience a similar breakthrough as regards the relationship between economics and social matters. The crucial breakthrough for this paradigm shift is now feasible due to the incredible success story of Grameen Bank, launched by Nobel Peace Prize laureate Prof. Muhammad Yunus, as well as his most recent global initiative, which he named "Social Business."

The GENISIS Institute for Social Business and Impact Strategies, "GENISIS Institute" for short, has made it its task to achieve a breakthrough for this fundamentally new approach. Nothing less than a new global social movement is to spring from this initiative, a "Global Entrepreneurs Network."

What is "Social Business?"

After his tremendous success with providing microfinance to the poorest of the poor — more than half a billion people have been freed from the poverty trap in this way — Yunus started a new global initiative in 2008. In addition to today's global economy, which is primarily driven by profits, he calls for the establishment of a second type of doing business. This is to create companies whose sole focus is on finding solutions to acute social and ecological problems and whose investors deliberately forgo any profits that go beyond securing the value of their investments. The profits of such companies should remain with the companies and be used to expand "social profit," which becomes the companies' corporate mission.

Yunus himself demonstrated how "Social Businesses" can function very successfully. In more than twenty of his own companies, in addition to his Grameen Bank, he showed how social companies can work substantially more effectively and more efficiently than traditional aid organisations and state-run development projects.

Social Businesses are extremely effective, because they follow clear economic principles and have to prove themselves in the marketplace. As a result, the ratio between resources input and desired output is optimised. While subsidised social or ecological projects require new supplies of money all the time, Social Businesses can do with start-up financing alone. Very many of the currently employed financial resources for such social tasks are released as a result and can be used for starting up a multiple of Social Businesses instead.

At the same time, though, Social Businesses are also highly efficient, i.e., they achieve a substantially higher level of social efficiency. This is closely linked to the "corporate philosophy" of Social Businesses. Social Business companies hire highly motivated and extremely professional people. In fact, they are motivated in two ways: by the decidedly meaningful activity and the challenge to prevail with that in the normal market. Another factor in increasing effectiveness is the issue of ownership: At least as far as the Grameen family of companies is concerned, these companies are not owned by an individual, or any other shareholders, but those who are affected. At Grameen Bank the poorest of the poor have a direct cooperative stake in the company and are thus also involved in its management and profits.

Let us now look at a Social Business in the Grameen family in an area that almost all experts from around the world had thought could not do without substantial international subsidies. "Grameen Shakti" ("Grameen Energy") distributes "Solar Home Systems," small solar-power plants that are installed next to a house or hut of an especially poor family and provide the electricity that such a family requires.

For a long time, development experts said that such solar plants did not make any economic sense, particularly in poverty regions. But here is what those experts overlooked: For the poorest of the poor, electricity is also nominally at its most expensive, because in the areas where they live there are usually no power lines. Therefore, they have to rely on extremely expensive sources of energy, such as batteries. "Grameen Shakti" offered its clients loans with which to buy Solar Home Systems, on the basis that they would pay back the loans in three years with the exact same monthly instalments that they had paid for their monthly electricity requirements. The only difference: These plants last for at least eight years. In other words, after three years, they can enjoy free electricity.

"Grameen Shakti" converted a subsidised sector to a functioning and booming Social Business. So far, 150,000 households in Bangladesh have bought such Solar Home Systems. Going by the current rate of growth, it is expected that it will be more than five million in Bangladesh alone by 2015. Given the ownership structure with respect to the plants, their owners have a markedly higher interest in maintaining them as well as their functionality. Even many women are eager to be trained as Solar Home Systems technicians so as to increase the systems' life even further.

But does this not involve a few potential economic sectors? And does this not tend to address primarily domestic companies, rather than western companies and groups? According to Yunus, a central area of Social Business is the creation of Social Joint Ventures.

The first company of global standing to set up a Social Joint Venture on the conditions described was the food company Danone. Danone boss Franck Riboud certainly did not do this only to burnish his company's image. His reasoning behind it was far more intelligent: A company that learns how to deal with development leading away from poverty sooner than its competitors thus acquires a competitive edge that cannot be overestimated.

"Grameen Danone," a company founded jointly by Grameen Bank and Danone AG, produces a special yoghurt that contains all the essential nutrients that the poorest of the poor normally lack. What is more, the entire production and distribution concept of this "joint venture to alleviate poverty practically" is designed such that its product is sold at a price far below that of all other yoghurts, which the poor were not able to afford.

By giving the poorest of the poor products that can actually pull them out of poverty, their needs will change with their economic development. There is no doubt either that they will never forget the companies they owe this help to. This is a highly efficient way of battling poverty and, at the same time, provides an opportunity for positioning in the markets of the future! "Once you have helped the poor to get out of poverty, you will be able also to position your profit-oriented companies in entirely new markets," Yunus called out to 70 CEOs of leading German companies at an event in April 2008. In the meantime, Yunus has seen a veritable wave of inquiries from large companies. The internationally renowned economist Prahalad sees in this the key to developing the largest and most interesting market of the future, that is, a market composed of two-thirds of humanity who are still largely locked out of the economy.

The GENISIS Institute positions itself as a think-and-do-tank for the paradigm shift described here, making the transition from charity-type thinking to social entrepreneurship, that is to say, towards the application of economic principles to social issues. In the area of "Social Business," the GENISIS Institute:

- identifies the models of social entrepreneurship all over the world that are particularly innovative, socially effective, successful and scalable;
- provides them with a platform of global conferences, such as the Vision Summit, as well as special education initiatives;
- initiates and supports the set-up of a strong infrastructure for Social Business, such as innovative financing instruments (Good Growth Fund, social exchanges, etc.);
- initiates cooperation between social companies and the business world in the spirit of Social Joint Ventures;
- studies jointly with experts and creative pioneers new implementation concepts for social entrepreneurship in Europe and around the world;
- and builds a "Global Entrepreneurs Network" of social companies.

All this is based on the close cooperation with a global network of especially successful social companies, ranging from Muhammad Yunus (Bangladesh) and Guenter Faltin (Germany) to Marcia Odell, who heads the Women's Empowerment Program in Africa.

GENISIS ensures the practical application of its impulses to specific projects, new social initiatives as well as new "Social Businesses" — by building and continuously improving a strong network of partners. Furthermore, the GENISIS Institute takes into account the fact that even such a powerful concept as Social Business may bump up against limits as long as the global general conditions of a global eco-social market economy have not been improved in a sustainable manner. To this end the GENISIS Institute is developing Global Impact Strategies together with other research institutes, which improve upon existing similar approaches like the Global Marshall Plan Initiative.

For the GENISIS Institute, Social Business is a fundamental further development of the concept of social entrepreneurship. So far, anything has been accepted as social entrepreneurship that contributes to solving social challenges in an innovative and scalable manner. Both these criteria also apply to Social Business, but Social Businesses also have to be economically sustainable as a result of their own strength. This was not a requirement for social entrepreneurship. Projects continuously funded through donations and subsidies were able to gain recognition under the label of social entrepreneurship. Social Business, however, represents an improved version of social entrepreneurship, allowing it to be economically functional. The GENISIS Institute sees in this systematic evolution of the social entrepreneurship approach one of its main tasks.

The GENISIS Institute was founded by nine entrepreneurs, social entrepreneurs and donors who are already successful players in this new sector of the global economy and who want to help to turn Social Business, with all the professionalism possible, into a new generation of a global social movement: People who want to address social issues should learn to implement such desire in entrepreneurial terms in the fullest sense of the word. People with a background in business should learn also to apply their skills directly to social issues. People who so far have been dependent recipients of aid more or less should be turned into self-confident "entrepreneurs of their own lives."

Entrepreneurs Creating the Economic Paradigm for the Future

*Paola Babos[1] and Monica Sharma[2] *,*
Leadership and Capacity Development, United Nations

> *A human being is part of the whole called by us the universe, a part limited in time and space. He experiences himself, his thoughts and feelings as something separated from the rest, a kind of optical delusion of his consciousness. This delusion is a kind of prison for us, restricting us to our personal desires and to affection for a few persons nearest to us. Our task must be to free ourselves from this prison by widening our circle of compassion to embrace all living creatures and the whole of nature in its beauty.*
>
> —*Albert Einstein*

Today we are living in a time of deep interdependence and seemingly great paradoxes. Never before have we had more abundant opportunities to fulfill people's needs worldwide. Each day we seamlessly move massive amounts of capital and other financial instruments around the globe. More than 100 million human beings cross borders and another 100 million move from rural to urban areas in search of opportunities. Information is constantly being generated and moved through cyberspace, connecting people globally and revolutionising our capacity to communicate and exchange across time and space. A new global culture is taking shape among the younger generation, often redefining the tastes, beliefs and values of local societies.

Yet in spite of the abundance of resources and technology available to us, the world economy teeters on the brink of a global economic breakdown. The deepening credit crisis in major developed market economies, triggered by the continuing housing slump, the declining value of the US dollar, persistent global imbalances and soaring commodity prices poses substantive threats to sustainable human development and well-being. Most shockingly, in a world economy that moves $2 trillion a day, we are witnessing the unfolding of a food crisis that is wholly man-made, with severe consequences for people across the world. Furthermore, we have been using the equivalent of 1.25 planets' worth of resources since 1997 resulting in the unsustainable use and degradation of nearly two thirds of ecosystem services[3].

The increasing instability of global markets and their reverberating effects on people across countries and continents underscore the limits of our current economic practices. The patterns underlying our current limits are mostly hidden from view. Even when we see them, we often do not know how to create an alternative. After each crisis we look back to identify its causes and identify ways to 'fix the mess' without ever really addressing the hidden underlying causes of their systemic nature and increasing frequency.

Why does our current economic model career from crisis to crisis when we supposedly have the most advanced technology and resources ever to satisfy human needs worldwide? What new approaches can we take on to reconstruct and transform economic practices for human and planetary well-being? To answer these questions, we explore what is missing in current economic thinking and practices, shedding light on what becomes possible in an economic structure that puts people at the centre of its design. We present examples of emerging economic practices that integrate equity with effectiveness and efficiency. Finally we look at how full-spectrum'[4] approaches sourced in people's transformational leadership and entrepreneurship can be applied at scale to see the emergence of a new entrepreneurship paradigm that maximises returns to society.

Seeing the Shared Context of Our Crises

Insanity is doing the same thing over and over
again and expecting different results.
            —*Rita Mae Brown*

You already know enough, so do I. It is not knowl-
edge we lack. What is missing is the courage to
understand what we know and to draw conclusions.
            —*Sven Lindquist*

In the age of global complexity, it is a common fallacy to think that there is little we can do in relation to the economic and social systems that have so far shaped our mutual relationships and existence on this planet. Mostly we get bogged down in ideological debates over the tangled web of tensions and contradictions that characterize the interaction of social and economic forces. For example, the technological and material progress we have made over the past decade is unprecedented in the history of humanity. The development of market economies has benefited large numbers of people over the past century, generating technological innovations that enhance life and human well-being. Conversely, the benefits of economic growth are increasingly skewed in favour of a small minority, and the nature and scale of production and consumption patterns is jeopardizing our very existence on this planet.

While the global economy has grown seven-fold since 1950, disparity in per capita gross domestic product between the 20 richest and 20 poorest nations more than doubled between 1960 and 1995. Today, of the 100 largest economies in the world, 59 are global corporations. Some 85% of the world's GDP is controlled by one fifth of the population. Even in the United States, home to the world's largest corporations, economic growth is becoming less able to foster human development across different income groups. The "Measure of America" report commissioned by Oxfam and several foundations[5] points to the dramatic decline of American society relative to other advanced industrialized countries and the mounting social disparities within the US. Of the world's 30 richest nations, the US has the highest proportion of children living in poverty, 15%. Income inequality gaps are stark: the average income of the top fifth of US households in 2006 was almost 15 times that of the lowest fifth (or $168,170 versus $11,352). The top 1% of households possesses at least 33% of the national wealth, while the bottom 60% possess just 4% of the total.

To understand why rising social and economic inequalities are at the heart of our current crises, we need to acknowledge that the dynamics of economic and social development are no longer determined primarily at the national and local level: they are nested in and informed by complex global systems. Global finance, international trade regimes, patenting rules and governance systems shape policy choices and freedoms across every country and community on the planet. They represent interconnected 'software nodes' that inform and organize the 'hardware' of production and distribution. The way in which we organize these nodes has a profound impact on our capacities to create meaningful systems of production and consumption to provide for people's needs and well-being.

For example, in the domain of finance, Hazel Henderson[6] has elo-quently explained over the years that while money has been an impor-tant invention in human societies, it only retains its value if it is a good tracking and scoring system of the products and exchanges of the real economy. Today we are witnessing the effects of massive credit creation in deregulated capital markets that fed the dot.com bubble of yesteryears, and the current housing, oil, and food crises. In essence, the deregulation of global finance has decoupled money from real wealth creation and 'market demand' from the actual needs of people.

Professor Michael Hudson at the Institute for the Study of Long Term Economic Trends traces the decoupling of money from real wealth to what he calls 'the magic of compound interest'[7]: that is, the tendency of debts to keep on doubling and redoubling through a complex set of market instruments in the finance, insurance and real estate sectors. Every rate of interest is a doubling time. No real economy's production and economic surplus can keep up with this tendency of debt to grow faster in a deregulated market.

The current strategy for wealth creation based on the global trading of complex financial products has unintended effects or costs. For example, leverage instruments such as complex derivatives use borrowed funds or debt to magnify or enhance the potential positive or negative outcome to increase the returns to equity. As the current financial crisis shows, after years of deregulation and inflated capital gains, leverage instruments have actually magnified systemic instability, mirroring the pitfalls of gambling strategies. Financial globalization has also fostered mergers and acquisi-tions on an unprecedented scale so that many of today's global corporations are larger than many governments. This has in turn hindered the financial viability of local small and medium size enterprises. As a result, deregula-tion of financial markets indirectly fosters polarization between those who live off the returns to wealth (that is, from the interest and rent extracted from finance and property and the capital gains derived from inflated asset prices) and those who live off what they can earn and who struggle to pay the taxes and debts they are encouraged to take on.

These unintended effects or costs are largely outside of our field of vision because national accounts – GNP and national income – do not distinguish how wealth is being created and distributed across the popu-lation. By the same token, our methods to track business performance have heretofore been limited to measuring return on investment and shareholder value. As a result, we fail to track the positive and negative externalities of productive systems on people and the planet.

In a brilliant 20-minute video titled 'Story of Stuff'[8], Annie Leonard maps what she calls the materials economy, showing the limits we are running up against, and some of the hidden social, economic and environmental externalities of a linear system in a finite planet that must be seen and urgently confronted.

- **Extraction**–Manufacturing is using up the planet's resources at an alarming rate. We have already consumed 33% of its resources. The US alone is using 30% of the world's resources despite having 5% of the world's population. If all countries were to consume at US rates, we would need 5 planets.
- **Production**–A 'profit above all' manufacturing strategy is wreaking havoc on our ecosystems and is responsible for climate change, water depletion, waste and toxic pollution. There are over 100,000 synthetic chemicals in use today, only a handful of which have been tested for individual, let alone synergistic impacts on health.
- **Distribution**–Once goods are produced, the main focus of distribution is to sell goods and services as quickly as possible, keeping prices down to increase sales volumes and keep the inventory moving. In a globalised world, price competition coupled with the drive to maximize profits means that manufacturers are externalizing production costs in a number of ways, including environmental pollution and exploitative labour practices, relocating factories and outsourcing jobs in order to pay the lowest wages.
- **Consumption**–The heartbeat of the entire system is a consumption culture that trains citizens to be avid consumers of goods and services by promising prestige, happiness, admiration, success and satisfaction. We see more advertisements in a year than our grandparents saw in their lifetime. We consume twice as much as 50 years ago, reversing values of thrift, resourcefulness and stewardship of the planet, in a paradigm where our consumption capacity defines our social status and value in society.
- **Disposal**–In the United States, 99% of purchased goods are disposed of within 6 months. In other words, American consumers have either used up or turned into garbage 30% of the world's resources. Recycling is therefore a necessary but not sufficient strategy for managing our resources and well-being.

In her vivid and succinct analysis, Annie Leonard examines how economic and social systems interact, pointing to the multiple limits we are facing. She shows that our patterns of production and consumption are unsustainable because they are not designed in the best interest of people and the planet. In fact we see that we live in a system in crisis, running a linear model on a finite planet, where people are the means of production and consumption, rather than the end of our economic engagement with each other and the world.

Figure 1
Systems and Results

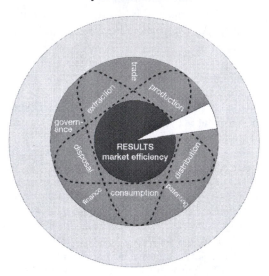

Figure 1 illustrates the logic of economic thinking and decision making today, where policies and regulatory environments in the domain of systems are geared to drive market efficiency and maximize returns in the inner domain of economic transactions.

What is evident is that people's best interest does not necessarily inform decision making in this approach. Our responses are partial: we design policies and organize systems according to market efficiency and shareholder returns, with no built-in mechanisms to track the impact of productive and regulatory systems on the well-being of people and the planet. In this model, we fail to ask a fundamental question: for what and for whom are we designing effective policies and efficient markets?

Without addressing these questions, market efficiency as measured by profit making becomes both the means and end of decision making for institutions, corporations and society at large. Economic practices therefore emphasize the short term over the long term; they focus on shareholders' return and largely fail to account for the social and environmental costs born by other stakeholders, or for the generations to come. As we discuss in the next section, our current measurements for economic growth reflect the partial nature of this approach, where non-monetized dimensions of human well-being are unaccounted for and fail to inform the policy and investment choices we make.

Investing in Human Agency and Well-Being as a Pathway to a Different Future

Wealth is evidently not the good we are seeking;
for it is merely useful and for the sake of something
else.

—*Aristotle*

Although we are apparently stuck in social, economic and political practices that are no longer working for the majority of people, cutting edge knowledge in the domains of physics and cognitive sciences, as well as real world social and economic applications, is showing us that innovation dynamics are fundamentally nested in human agency and expressed through social and interpersonal communication. Human agency is our capacity to make choices of our own, creating anew based on our deepest wisdom, insights and values, as distinct from the mere application of knowledge through 'either-or' constructs underpinning the scientific method.

Some economists are developing new frameworks focusing on a more holistic view of development that recognises the interaction between social and economic dimensions. Amartya Sen's work on the inter-relationship between development and freedom, Martha Nussbaum's work on ethics and human capabilities, and the applied research of the Oxford Poverty Human Development Initiative, led by Sabine Alkire, are some important contributions to this work. They see people as agents of development, "someone who acts and brings about change, and whose achievements can be judged in terms of her own values and objectives[9]."

Figure 2 reflects the missing domain of human agency, sourced in people's leadership and entrepreneurial spirit and manifested in actions that reflect our interdependence and human values. It shows that our capacity to generate sustainable patterns for personal and planetary well-being is nested in the domain of human agency. Human agency is the capacity to make choices and lead change. It is given by a set of human capabilities or functionings – expressed as 'beings', 'doings' and 'havings' – that a person can choose from and accomplish. This view generates a new context to understand and positively transform current patterns of economic engagement, enabling results that simultaneously address the triple bottom line: people, planet and profit. It moves us away from linear methods towards more holistic approaches to address complex global challenges.

Figure 2
Human Agency, Systems and Results

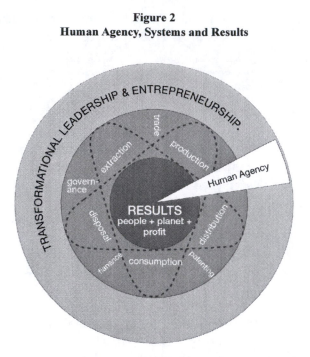

The hologram also shows that human freedoms – our individual and collective capacity to manifest human agency and expand our potential – are man made: they are partly determined and expressed through development policies, markets, and other social arrangements in the middle domain. We can therefore look at development as the extent to which social and economic arrangements expand human capabilities and freedoms.

Human well-being reflects a broader concept of development to include measures of life satisfaction, meaning and purpose[10], so that the material wealth we currently measure is complemented by dimensions of physical, mental and spiritual well-being (i.e. reflecting the range of human capabilities or functionings as 'beings', 'doings' and 'havings'). Some governments and institutions are exploring more holistic measures that reflect this approach in national accounting. Examples include Bhutan's Gross National Happiness[11] index; as well as efforts by the EU[12], Canada[13] and the OECD[14].

When policy making is guided by this broader concept of human well-being, our decision making processes reflect equity considerations necessary for expanding human capabilities. Equity refers to the distribution of economic and social benefits as they relate to universal principles of human dignity, respect for diversity/celebration of pluralism, non-discrimination, and interdependence. By including equity we acknowledge that the results of economic models and practices are not merely a function of market efficiency, but rest on ethical grounds related to the purposes we assign to markets, including distributional outcomes. When the purpose is articulated as human well-being, we can design effective policies and allocate resources efficiently in the best interest of people.

Nesting policy design in human agency allows us to generate alternatives in an iterative manner to shift economic institutions away from the injustices of stark inequalities, environmental destruction and debilitating boom and bust crises. With this as our aim, we can discover and institutionalise a new set of normative principles including social justice, equity, democracy, environmental sustainability and economic stability. This approach recognises the power of each of us to make choices that we value, engaging constructively with the world around us to reconstruct economic institutions in ways that are non-exploitative, non-destructive and stable.

Creating New Economic Practices

Profit is not the explanation, cause or rationale
of business behaviour and business decisions, but
rather the test of their validity.
                                                                        —*Peter Drucker*

A few thoughtful people from government, business and civil society are creating alternative economic practices recognising that people hold the experience, information and wisdom to generate sustainable solutions. They are asking piercing questions: "What forms of entrepreneurship foster human well-being across stakeholders? How can corporations truly perform on corporate social responsibility to deliver on the triple bottom line – people, planet and profit? If there are so many 'good' people with 'good' intentions, why don't we seem to make a dent in the world's problems?" Building on what is working in our practices, they integrate new strategies to maximise value to society.

Indeed, experience shows that we do not need to reinvent the wheel of economic institutions. For example, co-operatives[15] were developed to organise economic activities based on values of self-help, self-responsibility, democracy, equality, equity and solidarity starting in the 18th and 19th centuries. Today, modern co-operatives are business enterprises that extend ownership and control to stakeholders, including consumers, employees and members of the community in general. They serve purposes beyond profit maximisation: they openly and directly provide basic goods, financial services, education, housing and other goods and services to their members. By virtue of their governance principles[16] co-operatives are able to balance profit-making goals with other stakeholder needs. As the Mondragon Cooperative Corporation in Spain and the Federazione Trentina delle Cooperative in Italy show, it is possible to develop co-operative systems that are locally embedded to serve modern community needs and create value across stakeholders.

Today, co-operative enterprises and experiences have inspired the creation of new forms of business enterprises that combine social and economic goals. Some interesting examples include the development of Social Enterprises in Italy, of Community Interest Companies (CICs) in the UK and of BCorporations in the United States. These are innovative forms of for-profit companies that use new governance systems and strategies with the aim of generating profits while contributing to human well-being and social value. In the development arena, cooperative innovations include integrated models that combine fair trade, organic agriculture and microfinance.

And still this innovation remains partial. Cooperative movements around the world understand that – while these forms of economic and social innovation are important – their real strategic asset lays in the values and principles they stand for, not in the systemic innovations per se. As a result, they are looking for new methods and platforms that can empower people to understand the impact of global systems on local communities and generate new systemic expressions of cooperative values and principles.

Similarly, traditional businesses are learning from social enterprise models. Increasingly, they seek to maximise both economic and social returns serving all stakeholders. For example, Raj Sisodia, Jag Seth and David B. Woolfe define a new generation of companies that are maximising value to society - across communities and generations[17]. These humanistic companies – or Firms of Endearment (FoE) – are ultimate value creators: they create new types of capital through experiential value, social value, and of course, financial value. They find that publicly listed FoEs outperform the S&P 500 by significant margins over 10-, 5- and 3-year time horizons[18]. Similarly, in a 1992 study, Harvard Business School professors John Kotter and James Heskett studied the performance of 207 large U.S. companies in 22 different industries over a period of 11 years. They found that companies with strong business cultures that address all stakeholders and empower managers at all levels dramatically outperformed other companies by wide margins along three key indicators: revenue growth (682% versus 166%), stock-price increase (901% versus 74%) and net income increase (756% versus 1%)[19].

Innovations that focus on expanding human well-being are more than just sustainable: they respond to new market demands. Employees and consumers alike are looking for meaningful experiences. Businesses know talent is crucial to innovation. As a result they are creating new strategies to attract and retain the younger generation of workers. They look at the workplace as a way to constructively engage with the world: a vehicle to express their full potential, including values of diversity and global interdependence[20]. Responding to this, new business practices focus on respect for individuals, transparency and empowerment. They create workplaces that are fun, balanced and flexible, offering creative quality-of-life benefits.

Similarly, businesses recognize that creating new ethical standards is a win-win strategy – for consumers, shareholders, stakeholders and the environment. Conscious consumers demand ethical products that nurture life and generate positive externalities for people. They are also increasingly disillusioned with current business practices focusing on profit alone and determined to expose companies that are exploitative through information and action campaigns[21]. For example, a 2004 Yankelovich poll found that 80% of respondents believe business is too concerned about making a profit and not enough about responsibility to workers, consumers and the environment.

Finally, today's technological revolution is generating new opportunities for alternative business paradigms. Open source systems that foster participation create innovation at scale in a way that was not possible in the post-industrial paradigm. Effective businesses are now learning to tap into the prosumer paradigm of the internet 2.0 revolution[22] and develop new forms of organizations that generate value through reciprocity between producers and consumers.

In essence this emerging paradigm recognizes that we can either continue with business as usual, never really addressing what is not working in our current paradigm; or we can learn to do things differently, transforming risks to generate new business practices that honour people's leadership, fostering human well-being and development worldwide. Business leaders are strategically placed to address the systemic patterns that create the context of our lives. They recognize that when we take ownership of our current reality, we discover new entry points for action and the power of each of us to innovate and create value – as professionals, employees and consumers alike.

Designing Policies and Strategies for Human Well-Being at Scale

The world we have made as a result of the level of thinking we have done thus far creates problems that we cannot solve at the same level at which we have created them... We shall require a substantially new manner of thinking if humankind is to survive.

—*Albert Einstein*

These new economic practices are encouraging, and yet they often stand out as isolated cases. Innovative co-operatives, social enterprises, 'humanistic companies' and their counterparts in government and civil society understand this. They recognize that their key challenges rests in how to systematically activate human agency so as to generate alignment and resonance on universal values among members, employees, consumers, management, public authorities and local communities.

Drawing on both development and business experience, we are working with business leaders who are seeking to break new ground in this direction. Through the UN Leadership and Capacity Development Initiative we design programmes that develop deep transformational practices to align value maximization with universal principles and integrate values with technologies, as well as equity with efficiency. Our own experience sourcing development programmes in human agency shows that it is possible to distinguish, design and deliver policies and strategies that expand human capabilities, transform dysfunctional systems, and create alternative patterns of engagement at scale.

We refer to this programmatic approach as 'full-spectrum' (Figure 1), where learning-in-action methodologies are used a) to activate human agency through transformational leadership and entrepreneurship, b) address systems manifesting in societal and planetary transformation, and c) use appropriate technology that works for everyone[23]. The 'full-spectrum' hologram is a cognitive response map for programmatic design at scale.

In this paradigm, we recognize that the source of all action – both individual and collective (including systems) – is human agency, the capacity of people to lead change. Knowledge, technology and skills are necessary but not sufficient for designing and delivering effective

Figure 3
Full-spectrum design

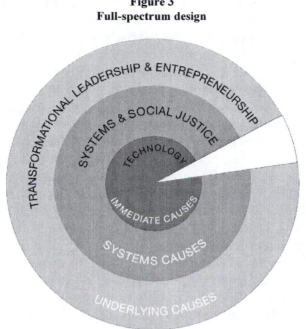

responses to complex global challenges. Rather, people's insights, information, experiences and resources are brought to bear in the design of responses, so that people everywhere are empowered to innovate and take action that systematically addresses complexity by understanding the underlying, intermediate and immediate causes of any given problem.

Just as we create strategies and policies to address systems issues, our experience shows that human agency and capabilities can be activated, nurtured and developed through leadership competencies, empowering people to be the change they want to see. Transformational leadership methods activate human agency by fostering Emotional Intelligence (EI) competencies[24] first researched and introduced into the business management lexicon by Daniel Goleman[25]. His research with more than 200 organisations around the world showed that EI matters twice as much as technical skills (IQ) in distinguishing high performance employees from mediocre-performing ones. In fact researchers have found that EI leads indirectly to competitive advantage because it is a prerequisite for the kind of leadership necessary to effect positive and sustainable strategic change[26].

Similarly, in '*Five Minds for the Future*', Harvard professor Howard Gardner[27] builds on his pathbreaking research on multiple intelligences to elaborate the kind of cognitive abilities (or 'minds') that will be critical to success in a 21st century. Beyond the disciplined and synthesizing minds, corresponding to the inner and middle domains, Gardner introduces three other minds – the creating, respectful and ethical minds – which reflect the domain of transformational leadership and entrepreneurship. They equip individuals with the possibility to break new ground, pose unfamiliar questions and put forth new ideas and fresh ways of thinking. These three capacities remain one step ahead of even the most sophisticated computers and robots as they align action with human values and personal ethics. Gardner underscores the importance of cultivating all five minds not just for individual development, but for tangible success in a full range of human endeavors, including education, business, science, art, politics and engineering.

Transformational leadership methods that integrate personal transformation with social transformation can be used to generate new results sourced from people's deepest wisdom. In other words, by learning to use our full cognitive and leadership capacities we can think anew and create new patterns of economic and social engagement for human well-being at scale. Learning-in-action methodologies pioneered for development action through the Leadership for Results Programme on HIV/AIDS of the United Nations Development Programme (UNDP) generated extraordinary results, reaching 130 million people with over five thousand breakthroughs in 40 countries[28]. This work built on the successes of UNICEF's earlier maternal mortality reduction programme in six countries in South Asia[29].

The corporate world offers examples of innovations sourced from transformational leadership that have successfully addressed the triple bottom line – profit, people and planet. In South Africa, for example, Lonmin (a primary producer of Platinum Group Metals) has pioneered transformational processes and standards engaging all stakeholders – management, trade unions and stakeholder communities – to address the prospective closure of one of its mines. Using leadership competencies the strategy addressed critical issues of racial diversity and poverty, generating a new context and future for the mine workers, their relationship with management and their communities. In India, iDiscoveri works with the education sector and has designed programmes and platforms that integrate leadership in education and management, serving both corporations and public schools[30]. There are a few examples in

Enterprise 2021

INSPIRING LEADERSHIP

1. Led and managed by 'personally aware' individuals, who can distinguish systemic patterns and operate from 'ground of being'
2. Values human dignity, delivering high quality social and economic alternatives for all people, including the marginalized

WHOLE-SYSTEM ORGANISATION

3. Is sustainable as a whole system (across the value-chain and stakeholders)
   a. Managerially – as sourced in people's generative capacity
   b. Financially – combining wealth creation/profit while simultaneously contributing to humanity as a strategic choice
   c. Technologically –integrating technology with transformation and human dignity
   d. Environmentally – honouring the planet and all of life and nature in its beauty

TRANSFORMATIVE STRATEGIES FOR EFFECTIVE CREATION

4. Is able to distinguish, design and deliver full spectrum responses related to (i) people, (ii) products, and (iii) process
5. Is fully aware of global/national/local systems and capable of leveraging them to create full spectrum alternatives that empower others and generate 'win-win' solutions
6. Generates space of resonance- where other Enterprise 2021 seed and thrive
7. Actively pursues pathways of excellence to support, finance and sustain Enterprise 2021

INSIDE-OUT RESULTS FOR SUSTAINABILITY AND EQUITY

8. Is a 'stage 5' organization*:
   a. Healthy management: expanding human capabilities through personal transformation, participation, and mastery in a specific domain
   b. Principled leadership: the ability to influence without authority and generate results, with integrity/accountability/responsibility
   c. Embodies core principles and creates an enabling environment for human dignity, non discrimination, equity, and non violence,
   d. Recognizes interdependence and values diversity: the ability to see different perspectives, providing a space for creating alternatives and innovation

---

* 'Stage 5' relates to the 'developmental stages of organizations' as they apply to managers, leaders, groups and organizations: Dennis Emberling (www.developmentalconsulting. com) and Allan Henderson, 'Commitment-in-action Programme', GHJ Consulting, 2005.

civil society organisations, such as Ashoka Foundation, where personal transformation manifests in significant transformation, and where interior deeper-rooted forces are addressed along with systems and technological approaches.

Moving To A New Organisational Paradigm: Enterprise 2021

Creating a new entrepreneurship paradigm that generates new patterns sourced in 'full-spectrum' design requires an evolution in organizational development to foster synergy and resonance across sectors, activities and communities. The focus is on taking a long term perspective where revenue and value is generated not only for shareholders, but also for all stakeholders – integrating values and principles with new systemic patterns across employees, their communities, suppliers and distributors, and the world at large.

Enterprise 2021 is a learning-in-action organisation that displays emotionally intelligent leadership, commitment to exemplary citizenship and recognition that it is part of an economic ecosystem with many interdependent participants. It delivers full spectrum strategies and innovations for systems transformation, generating spaces of resonance for principled action grounded in universal human values across people, processes and products. The examples detailed in the previous section represent organizations moving in this direction.

Enterprise 2021 is sustained by inside-out practices, where all actors and stakeholders are empowered to walk the talk and create change that works for everyone. The CEO is personally engaged in generating new strategies sourced in people's wisdom. Enterprise 2021 generates results along the triple bottom line by using transformational approaches that activate human agency and principled action among all players -governing boards, trade unions, shareholders, stakeholders, public authorities and communities. Learning-in-action platforms are designed to encourage innovations and breakthrough initiatives within and outside the company fostering personal engagement and commitment. Community service and corporate social responsibility is then transformed from a public relations instrument to the source of meaningful engagement by management, employees and stakeholders, where partnership is not simply 'technical support' for local civil society organisations, but the opportunity for one's own growth and contribution.

In this way, Enterprise 2021 creates urgency for positive action that generates social and personal value. It opens new pathways to address "systems issues" pioneering new standards within the industry and charting alternatives that impact the "triple bottom-line": people-planet-profit.

Entrepreneurship That Works for Everyone

Global civil society and thousands of organizations and institutions worldwide have already committed to action sourced in our individual and collective wisdom through the creation of the Earth Charter[31]. Making that vision come alive for a sustainable future requires a paradigm shift in our current economic approaches, supported by new forms of organizations. Some of us are finding the courage to address difficult choices and find ways to harmonize diversity with unity, the exercise of freedom with the common good, short-term objectives with long-term goals. Are you a full-spectrum entrepreneur, a pattern maker of a different kind, bridging personal transformation manifests societal transformation? Every individual, family, organization, and community has a vital role to play:

- Are you a policymaker or elected representative who sees the power of human agency for generating sustainable wealth creation and human well-being? How do you design policy frameworks and organize services to sup-port the expansion of human freedoms and capabilities?
- Are you an economist, financial analyst or statistician, who seeks to urgently integrate equity with effectiveness and efficiency so that social and economic arrangements expand human capabilities? What new measures and indices are you using to track human agency and well-being?
- Are you a leader in your industry who can distinguish, design and deliver full-spectrum responses that generate innovation sourced from the creative space of the people you lead and the processes you change? What new standards are you generating to deliver along the triple bottom line and maximize value to society as a whole?
- Are you a consultant who addresses complex global, national and subnational systems and their consequences for people and the planet? What tools are you using to empower people, organizations and institutions to generate social and economic alternatives that combine equity with efficiency and effectiveness?
- Are you an entrepreneur pioneering a new paradigm such as 'Enterprise 2021'? What platforms and approaches are you using to develop people's leadership and capabilities so that your organization delivers innovation across the triple bottom line?

Today we stand at a historical crossroad: we can continue to muddle through, from one crisis to the next, or we can chose to transform today's crises to seek a new beginning and a different trajectory for human evolution. In the face of global instability and insecurity, we have the opportunity to declare that this is enough – that we are more than mere means of development and exchange in a global marketplace. We can learn to trust the power of human agency and wisdom to create a different future, allowing new patterns to unfold so that we can embrace our essential oneness and realize our full potential. The choice is ours.

*   The opinions expressed in this article are those of the authors, and do not necessarily reflect the policies or views of the United Nations.

The authors gratefully acknowledge **Ronald Critchlow** for insightful comments and suggestions, and **Uriel Ortega** for designing the diagrams and asking thought provoking questions.

Notes

1. Paola Babos, Programme Officer, Leadership and Capacity Development, United Nations
2. Monica Sharma, M.D., Director, Leadership and Capacity Development, United Nations
3. www.millenniumassessment.org
4. A response a) sourced in wisdom, b) recognizing patterns and creating alternatives, and c) generating concrete measurable results. See Monica Sharma, "From Personal to Planetary Transformation", in Kosmos, Fall/Winter 2007.
5. See http://measureofamerica.org
6. See www.ethicalmarkets.com
7. See http://www.michael-hudson.com
8. www.storyofstuff.com
9. Amartya K. Sen, op.cit., p. 19
10. Gallup, State of Global Well-Being 2007
11. See http://www.grossinternationalhappiness.org
12. See http://www.beyond-gdp.eu
13. See http://www.gpiatlantic.org
14. For more information see OECD, The Global Project on Measuring the Progress of Societies, at http://www.oecd.org/pages/0,3417,en_40033426_40033828_1_1_1_1_1,00.html
15. A co-operative is defined as an autonomous association of persons united voluntarily to meet their common economic, social and cultural needs and aspirations through a jointly-owned and democratically-controlled enterprise.
16. These include: voluntary and open membership; democratic member control; member economic participation; autonomy and independence; education training and information; co-operation among co-operatives; and concern for community.
17. Raj Sisodia, Jag Seth and Davide B. Wolfe, Firms of Endearment: The Pursuit of Purpose and Profit, Wharton School Publishing, 2007.
18. Over the 10 years ending June 30, 2006, public FoEs returned 1,026 percent for investors, compared to 122 percent for the S&P 500: more than an 8:1 ration. Ibid., p. 16
19. John Kotter and James Heskett, Corporate Culture and Performance, Free Press, 1992.

20. Edward E. Lawler III, "The Talent Lie", Strategy+Business Magazine, www.strategy-business.com/press/article/08204?gko=45947-1876-26908103&tid=230&pg=all
21. Raj Sisodia, Jag Seth and Davide B. Wolfe, op.cit., p.24
22. Don Tapscott and Anthony D. Williams, Wikinomics: How Mass Collaboration Changes Everything, Portfolio, New York, 2006.
23. For a more detailed discussion of the 'full-spectrum' approach, see Monica Sharma, "From Personal to Planetary Transformation", in Kosmos, Fall/Winter 2007.
24. Emotional Intelligence (EI) competencies include four sets of leadership competencies: self-awareness, self-management, social awareness, and relationship skills
25. Daniel Goleman, Emotional Intelligence, Bantam Books, 1995, New York; and Daniel Goleman, Richard Boyatzis, and Anne McKee, Primal Leadership: Realizing the Power of Emotional Intelligence, Harvard Business School Press, 2002, Cambridge, Mass.
26. Ranjit Voola, Jamie Carlson, and Andrew West (2004), "Emotional Intelligence and Competitive Advantage: Examining the Relationship for a Resource-based View," in Strategic Change, Mar/Apr, Volume 13, Issue 2, pp.83-93.
27. Howard Gardner was named one of the top five influential business thinkers by the Wall Street Journal in a major feature titled "New Breed of Business Gurus Rises" on May 5th 2008.
28. Monica Sharma, 'Conscious Leadership at the Crossroads of Change', Shift Magazine, n.12, September-November 2006
29. See UNICEF, Saving Women's Lives: a call to rights-based action, UNICEF Regional Office for South Asia, 2000.
30. See http://www.idiscoveri.com
31. See www.earthcharter.org

Transformative Entrepreneurship from a Global and Integral Perspective

Nancy Roof, Kosmos Associates-Kosmos Journal

WORLD IN TRANSITION: ENDINGS AND BEGINNINGS

An entrepreneurial spirit of momentous proportions is exploding in every field of human endeavor. The world is ripe for change. Never before in our lifetimes have so many seen first hand the injustice and misery in the world, had the freedom to envision a new world, and been skilled enough to create a sustainable civilization worthy of the dignity of all Life.

We are experiencing endings and new beginnings at the same time. In times of transformation the art of 'letting go' becomes as important as the entrepreneurship to create the new. Why is social and transformational entrepreneurship on the rise now?

There is widespread recognition that we are living in a time of transition between two eras. Some are calling it the Second Enlightenment as we begin to realize that the scale of accelerating change is of transformational proportions. As technology brings us closer to one global community the new science of interdependence confirms are interconnectedness. We are being pushed by the realization of the full impact of the damage we have done by exploiting the resources of the planet and our inability to live in harmony with each other threatening the survival of our species. Our inner lives are impoverished as well with growing alienation and fragmentation, the devaluing of feminine values of caring and concern and emotional connections. We are the first generation to know the extent of the world's injustices and misery through new technologies that bring this reality into our living rooms. It is within this context that a new spirit is rising.

When old ways do not work anymore, transformational entrepreneurs rise with new and creative ideas that can shape a new civilization. Their generative creativity solves the problems of the old and creates a whole new worldview and institutions that match.

Rise Of Global Civil Society

In the past we relied on governments to solve our problems. We handed our power over to them believing that they represented our interests. We felt secure because we thought that the United Nations would solve our global problems. We looked to traditional sources of philanthropy to provide the financial backing for innovative projects we knew were important and would surely be sufficiently financed. These institutions no longer suffice to address the complexity of the global challenges we face today. Democratic global governance is lacking as nations continue to compete with each other rather than cooperate for the common good. Trust in governments and corporate power is at an all time low. In a world of accelerated change, central planning and decisions made now for future generations to fulfill are outdated before they become a reality. This kind of 'distance' decision-making loses its vitality and inhibits the kind of entrepreneurial spirit necessary for sustainable change.

Hierarchical systems are beginning to collapse in favor of decentralized power in the West and with it increased freedom to innovate. International civil society stepped into the vacuum in the 90s and began to coordinate efforts through major United Nations Conferences. We might say that collective global entrepreneurship emerged at that time. The founding of the International Criminal Court and the movement to outlaw landmines were two of the major accomplishments of the Collective working together. In the 21st century more integration occurred as the most successful global endeavors involve partnerships between governments, civil society, and business. A promising entrepreneurial effort by James Quilligan and Frithof Finkbeiner to coalesce global civil society into a major force for global change is called the Coalition for the Global Commons.

Rise of Global Philanthropists

We need a whole new relationship to philanthropy – and entrepreneurs are leading the way. My experience doing humanitarian work in the former Yugoslavia during the Balkans War was a real eye-opener. To my astonishment many groups designed their projects to meet the limiting requirements of grant-making foundations in order to be financed rather than meeting the needs of the desperate people. The result was numerous overlapping and repeated projects. Other groups flew into the war-zones in the morning – took photos of their landing and quickly took off. Mission accomplished! Fortunately some enlightened foundations, such as Kalliopeia are stepping into the vacuum where the importance of interior values and processes of change are recognized and quality is given precedence over quantity.

Bill Gates is one of several successful business entrepreneurs who is transitioning into global social entrepreneurship. Ted Turner and George Soros are early global philanthropic entrepreneurs who have had a world-wide impact through the United Nations and world economics.

Rise of New Consciousness and Values

Those who grasp the emerging future have expanded their values to global, universal, inclusive, evolutionary and transformational levels. Care and responsibility for all humanity is rapidly expanding beyond national boundaries. Studies of Western values indicate a steady movement away from materialism and status-seeking toward those for the common social good. A movement honoring Generosity of Spirit is beginning to arise spearheaded by such people as Michael Lerner, founder of the Spiritual Progressives, Nipun Mehta at CharityFocus and Pamela Hawley at UniversalGiving.

Entrepreneurs of the inner life and values that have had global impact include Barbara Marx Hubbard a pioneer in global consciousness; Jean Houston and Monica Sharma bringing inner and outer approaches to new global leadership; Ken Wilber, integral philosopher; Don Beck, founder of macro-psychology and Spiral Dynamics Integral; Ervin Laszlo, one of the first to merge science and consciousness towards a new civilization; the global humanitarian Prince El Hassan of Jordan marrying inner spirituality with global action for the global commons; Desmond Tutu, founder of successful forgiveness between nations; Kamran Mofid, founder of Globalization for the Common Good, expanding the understanding of globalization beyond transnational corporations; and many more. New spirituality arising with such groups as Global New Thought, marry the inner world of personal change with the outer world of service. In 1994 the foundational nature of values and spirituality was recognized at the United Nations and we co-founded the Values Caucus in 1994 with the help of Ambassador Somavia, now Director-General of the International Labor Organization, and in 2000 the Spiritual Caucus.

Rise of Global Social Entrepreneurs: The Hope of the World

Social entrepreneurs are a new and major force for global change. The term was coined in the mid 80s by Bill Drayton, one of America's top 25 leaders, according to *US News & World Report*. He founded Ashoka, the premier organization promoting Social Entrepreneurship worldwide. According to Drayton, "Social entrepreneurs are individuals with innovative solutions to society's most pressing social problems. They are ambitious and persistent, tackling major social issues and offering new ideas for wide-scale change."

"Social entrepreneurs have the hope, vision and power to change the world," says David Bornstein, author of *How to Change the World*. They are "driven, creative individuals who question the status quo, exploit new opportunities, refuse to give up and remake the world for the better." Largely unreported by the media, the nonprofit sector is the fastest growing segment of society, he says. Millions of ordinary people are stepping in to solve many of the world's most intractable problems.

Jeff Skoll, founder and chairman of Skoll Foundation for social entrepreneurs says, "Human progress has always been led by visionary individuals who seek a better future and dedicate their lives to realizing that promise. These social entrepreneurs tackle some of the world's toughest challenges with grit and determination." As society's change agents, they are pioneers of "innovation that benefits humanity and has a positive impact on the world."

Exceptional people have always existed as beacons of hope. Social entrepreneurs like Mahatma Gandhi, Florence Nightingale, and Mother Theresa are known worldwide. We admire them because they are exceptional and rare. Today there is a massive emergence of individuals and groups with a global mission of world benefit. They are becoming a powerful third force, along with business and governments, with substantial potential influence to change the world.

Kosmos Journal tracks social entrepreneurs and identifies many of the outstanding individuals and groups who are transformational entrepreneurs, leading the way toward the emerging new civilization. They envision some new enterprise and accept full responsibility for its outcome. They shift perceptions, change mind-sets and values. They are self-aware and understand the gift they have to offer while recognizing right timing for its realization. Their passion leads them forward with strength. Courage and persistence overcome inner doubt and outer blockages. They are usually impelled with an inner sense of a mission they were born to serve... And this mission becomes unstoppable.

They arise spontaneously in most cases, driven by an inner calling or out of outrage over gross injustices or the great suffering of a broken heart. Lack of time and funds are often overridden with determination and will. Because of their generous spirit and love they express constant and deep gratitude for the privilege of being able to serve—the gratitude that comes from living a life of consequence that makes a difference. Their goal is to give laser-like focus to the inner calling they must fulfill for the sake of humanity. They understand that they have only one piece of the whole puzzle and are a leader in that area only and a follower in others. Integrity, trustworthiness and transparency are their most important traits. They are free to go against the tide because they are not drive by the need for money and status.

The success of the enterprise has more to do with the strength of the inner intention of the leader than with the idea itself. When the entrenched interests of those who benefit from the status quo confront a new idea, it is clear that good ideas and being 'right' are not enough.

Many of the entrepreneurs I know who are making a global impact are driven by a strong spirituality and understand the need to change themselves in order to change the world. Little destructive habits of thought can diminish our resolve with doubts and fears and strong emotions can strain our capacity to be centered. We are most courageous when we know we are part of something much larger than ourselves. With spiritual development the urge to serve, to take responsibility and to make a difference becomes compelling.

An Integral Approach to Transformation Entrepreneurship

We at *Kosmos* Journal have discovered that a comprehensive or integral approach is necessary to realize sustainable global transformation in an increasingly complex world. The integral approach recognizes four interdependent dimensions involved with any transformation: the inner life of individuals, their outer behavior, collective worldviews or culture, and outer institutional systems. In the past we have tended to recognize one or two dimensions only, thus taking a partial approach to change. Most often in global circles we find an emphasis on the outer dimensions of politics, economics and law, and a lack of understanding about the importance of inner values, mindsets, attitudes and worldviews that are the foundation of any sustainable development.

The power of the interior dimension is unrecognized in many of the power elite of the world. Development and humanitarian aid often fails because of a lack of understanding that different mindsets and worldviews are the invisible cause of surface behavior. Time and again individuals and countries have exacerbated conflict thinking they were doing the 'right' thing for the other.

We have no trouble recognizing improvements and changes in developing countries where such groups are managing food, water, and life sustaining necessities as Ashoka so successfully illustrates. Unfortunately we tend to look at the outside of problems before recognizing the inner worldviews and mindsets that create many of the challenges the global community now faces.

In addition, the integral approach recognizes that all life is evolving and changing. All human life, cultures, nature, even the universe are processes rather than nouns or fixed things. Further, research indicates that the trajectory of evolution is towards larger wholes and the harmony and oneness of all life. Further, the integral approach recognizes the diverse deep structural value systems that underlie surface behavior.

Global Entrepreneur, Don Beck, founder of Spiral Dynamics Integral and Global Macro Psychology, is developing natural designs in many countries including Palestine with his talented assistant, Elza. His natural designs are based on discovering the emerging future based on deep listening to the needs of the people involved. Most important in his work is understanding the evolution of deeply ingrained value systems formed as a result of different life circumstances. Tracing the evolution of culture we find stages of development from survival, to tribal, to heroic, to traditional, to modern, to postmodern and integral. Without a consideration of these stages of development we can and have imposed our own experience and solutions on others. In developing countries we find tribal and heroic consciousness dominates. In Western society we find traditionalist, modern scientific materialism, and postmodern inclusive values – and sometimes integral with a global vision. These clashing worldviews account for many of the conflicts we experience today. Networks, partnerships, dialogues, listening skills and natural designs are needed to manage these differences as we move into the new civilization.

The Power of an Innovative Evolutionary Idea, Motivated by Love, Fulfilled with an Invincible Will

For me it all began with an amazing inner experience rather than an evolutionary idea. I was privy to early information about the genocide perpetrated in the former Yugoslavia of thousands of innocent people just like you and me. I was overcome with grief and felt helpless to change the situation. I then had an amazing inner experience, which I shall never forget. It was much bigger than compassion and caring. It was a huge inner explosion breaking my heart that had expanded to embrace the world-heart. I suffered for each innocent victim of the atrocity although I had never actually met any of them. I knew nothing about the former Yugoslavia except that a great injustice was happening. My inner world called me in the most powerful way to learn – and I did. Using my own finances I traveled to the war zone and interviewed dozens of people and organizations, asking the question. What do you need? The trauma and stress lived daily by the service providers proved unbearable and disabling. The innovative idea came directly from the people themselves who told me what they needed. The victims of war extended to families and caretakers—creating untold mental damage reaching way beyond the direct victims. We were in virgin territory. Attention had never been given to the secondary effects showered on families and service providers of direct victims. Despite all odds we found a way to set up the first training programs in a war-zone for service providers suffering from secondary traumatic stress.

My story is repeated over and over again by the newly arising social entrepreneurs for humanity. Nancy Rivard was driven by compassion for orphaned children and unmet humanitarian needs she discovered while traveling worldwide as an airline hostess. She thought, "Why not utilize empty areas of airplanes to bring medicines and aid to those in need?" Moved by a broken heart and inspired by an innovative idea, she established the amazing Airline Ambassador program. She has received several awards in recognition of her entrepreneurial service that has hand-delivered $42 million in aid to 52 countries.

Another friend of Kosmos, Amber Chand, lived in a refugee camp for part of her childhood. She now runs a entrepreneurial business selling beautiful handicrafts made by women in refugee camps who have no other way of earning income.

John Marks had a powerful idea and he was skilled enough to put it into action. He asked, "What we related to each other through our commonalities rather than our differences?" Search for Common Ground was the result, now serving thousands in 17 countries with a $13 million budget.

It is inspiring to know that every single person has the potential to change the world for the better– and many already have. Peter Drucker says, "Whenever anything is being accomplished, it is being done by a monomaniacal with a mission." And that is what the social entrepreneur in each of us is.

Individuals and groups of people with an innovative idea, compassionate love of humanity and animated by an invincible will are the hope of the world. We are just beginning to see the immense power of this triple combination to effect worldwide change. The entrepreneurial spirit in each of us may well be what saves us all.

Part B

Social Entrepreneurship:
Rise of an Innovative Citizen Sector

Everyone a Changemaker –
Social Entrepreneurship's Ultimate Goal*

Bill Drayton, Ashoka: Innovators for the Public

Rodrigo Baggio grew up in Rio de Janeiro loving computers. As he matured into an extraordinarily tall, thin man with a hugely wide smile, he became a computer consultant. However, from early on, he was one of the few in his generation who noticed – with concern – that the young people growing up in the favelas on the hills overlooking his middle-class neighborhood had no access to this digital world.

Because he has the great entrepreneur's tenacity of observation and thought as well as action, he decided he had to take on the digital divide – well before the phrase came into currency – and he has been pursuing this vision relentlessly ever since. While beginning to work toward this dream as a teenager, he learned just how motivated and capable of learning the young people in the favelas were. And also how competent the favela community was in organizing.

This respect underlies the central insight that has allowed Rodrigo to have a growing multi-continental impact. Rodrigo provides only what the community cannot: typically computers, software, and training. The community does the organizing, finding space, recruiting the students and faculty, and providing ongoing administration. The result is a uniquely economical model, and also one which, because the investment strengthens the broader community, it is self-sustaining and a foundation for other initiatives long into the future.

Rodrigo's chain of hundreds of community-based computer training schools now serves hundreds of slums across Latin America and Asia. These schools now have 700,000 graduates.

I got a sense of Rodrigo's power when he came to Washington shortly after being elected an Ashoka Fellow. Somehow he convinced the Inter-American Development Bank to give him its used (but highly valuable) computers. Somehow he convinced the Brazilian Air Force first to warehouse and then to fly these computers home. And then he somehow managed to persuade the Brazilian customs authority to allow all these computers in at a time when Brazil was trying to block computer imports.

Several years later, I got a further sense of how his mind worked, when I asked him why he was starting his work in Asia in Japan. Japan, he said, was the only large Asian source of computers where he could imagine getting people to give them to him. Therefore, as his first step, he had to demonstrate the value of his program to the Japanese in several of their own slums.

That is how entrepreneurs work. Having decided that the world must change in some important way, they simply find and build highways that lead inexorably to that result. Where others see barriers, they delight in finding solutions and in turning them into society's new and concrete patterns.

That much is easy to observe. However, there is more to it. Somehow, an unknown, young, lanky Rodrigo, the head of a new and unknown citizen organization, persuaded the managers of one after another of society's big institutions to do things they never would have imagined. He knew they were the right and logical things to do. Somehow they sensed that inner confidence and found it surprisingly persuasive.

What were they sensing? Rodrigo's words and arguments no doubt helped, but few people are willing to step out beyond the safely conventional merely on the basis of good arguments. Rodrigo was persuasive because his listeners sensed something deeper.

What Rodrigo was proposing was not just an idea, but the central logic of his life –as it is for every great entrepreneur. He mastered and came to love the new digital world from the time he was a young boy. More important, his values from early on drove him to care about the poverty and inequality he could see on the hillsides rising behind the middle-class Rio in which he was growing up. His values and his temperament had him taking on the digital divide before the term was invented.

As a result, when Rodrigo sat across the table from the much older, powerful officials he needed to move, they were confronting not just a good idea, but deeply rooted and life-defining values: non-egoistic, kindly determination and commitment.

This values-based faith is the ultimate power of the first-class entrepreneur. It is a quality others sense and trust, whether or not they really fully grasp the idea intellectually. Even though they would not normally want to step out in front of the crowd, a quiet voice tells them to trust Rodrigo and go with his vision.

Any assessment of Rodrigo's impact that stopped with his idea, let alone his business plan, would not have penetrated to the core of his power. Our field has been impoverished by too many assessments that never get to the essence.

Nor is Rodrigo's most important impact his schools or the life-changing independence and mastery he provides his students. Consider the impact Rodrigo has on a community when he introduces his program. It is not a school created by the government or outsiders. It is a school created by, funded by, managed by, and staffed by people in the community. The students are responsible for learning and then making their way. Think how many patterns and stereotypes are crumpled by these simple and very obvious facts. The psychological impact is a bit like India emerging from 50 years of falling behind to suddenly being recognized as the new challenger at the cutting edge of the most advanced part of the world's economy.

Accompanying this disruption of old patterns of action and perception is another contribution, and I believe it is the greatest one of Rodrigo and every entrepreneur: the idea of catalyzing new local changemakers into being. Unless the entrepreneur can get someone in one community after another to step forward and seize his or her idea, the entrepreneur will never achieve the spread that is essential to his or her life success. Consequently, the entrepreneur presents his or her idea to the local community in the most enticing, safe, understandable, and user-friendly ways possible.

Of course, the entrepreneur's own life story is in itself a beacon encouraging hundreds of others to care and to take initiative. This also increases the number of local changemakers. Moreover, when these local champions then build the teams they need to launch the idea they have adopted, they are providing not only encouragement but also training to potential next-generation local changemakers.

As the field of social entrepreneurship has grown and multiplied and wired itself together across the globe over the last 25 years, the rate of this plowing and seeding at the local level has accelerated dramatically. Ten years ago, the probability of an idea from Bangladesh affecting a community in Brazil, Poland, or the U.S. was very limited. Now it is common (the best-known example being Muhammad Yunus's impact on the global spread of microcredit) and be coming more common every year.

As the number of leading pattern-changing social entrepreneurs has been increasing everywhere, and as the geographic reach of their ideas has been expanding ever more rapidly, the rate of plowing and seeding therefore has multiplied. As have the number of local changemakers.

This whole process is enormously contagious. As the number of large-scale entrepreneurs and local changemakers multiplies, so does the number of support institutions, all of these make the next generation of entrepreneuring and changemaking easier. Not only do people not resist, but in fact, they respond readily to this change. Who wants to be an object when they could be changemakers, when they could live lives far more creative and contributory and therefore respected and valued?

As important as Rodrigo's impact is on the digital divide and on the lives and communities he serves, I believe this second dimension of his impact is far more important – especially at this transitional moment in history.

The most important contribution any of us can make now is not to solve any particular problem, no matter how urgent energy or environment or financial regulation is. What we must do now is increase the proportion of humans who know that they can cause change. And who, like smart white blood cells coursing through society, will stop with pleasure whenever they see that something is stuck or that an opportunity is ripe to be seized. Multiplying society's capacity to adapt and change intelligently and constructively and building the necessary underlying collaborative architecture, is the world's most critical opportunity now. Pattern-changing leading social entrepreneurs are the most critical single factor in catalyzing and engineering this transformation.

Everyone A Changemaker

The agricultural revolution produced only a small surplus, so only a small elite could move into the towns to create culture and conscious history. This pattern has persisted ever since: only a few have held the monopoly on initiative because they alone have had the social tools.

That is one reason that per capita income in the West remained flat from the fall of the Roman Empire until about 1700.

By 1700, however, a new, more open architecture was beginning to develop in northern Europe: entrepreneurial/competitive business facilitated by more tolerant, open politics. The new business model rewarded people who would step up with better ideas and implement them, igniting a relentlessly expanding cycle of entrepreneurial innovation leading to productivity gains, leading to ever more entrepreneurs, successful innovation, and productivity gains.

One result: the West broke out from 1,200 years of stagnation and soon soared past anything the world had seen before. Average per capita income rose 20 percent in the 1700s, 200 percent in the 1800s, and 740 percent in the last century.

The press reported the wars and other follies, but for the last 300 years this profound innovation in how humans organize themselves has been the defining, decisive historical force at work.

However, until 1980, this transformation bypassed the social half of the world's operations. Society taxed the new wealth created by business to pay for its roads and canals, schools and welfare systems. There was no need to change. Moreover, no monopoly, public or private, welcomes competition because it is very likely to lose. Thus, the social sector had little felt need to change and a paymaster that actively discouraged it.

Hence, the squalor of the social sector. Relative performance declining at an accelerating rate. And consequent low repute, dismal pay, and poor self-esteem and élan.

By the nineteenth century, a few modern social entrepreneurs began to appear. The anti slavery leagues and Florence Nightingale are outstanding examples. But they remained islands.

It was only around 1980 that the ice began to crack and the social arena as a whole made the structural leap to this new entrepreneurial competitive architecture.

However, once the ice broke, catch-up change came in a rush. And it did so pretty much all across the world, the chief exceptions being areas where governments were afraid.

Because it has the advantage of not having to be the pioneer, but rather of following business, this second great transformation has been able steadily to compound productivity growth at a very fast rate. In this it resembles successful developing countries like Thailand.

Ashoka's best estimate is that the citizen sector is halving the gap between its productivity level and that of business every 10 to 12 years. This rapidly rising productivity means that the cost of the goods and services produced by the citizen sector is falling relative to those produced by business – reversing the pricing pattern of the last centuries that led to the much-criticized "consumer" culture.

As a result, as resources flow into the citizen sector, it is growing explosively. It is generating jobs two and a half to three times as fast as business. There are now millions of modern, competing citizen groups, including big, sophisticated second-generation organizations, in each of the four main areas where the field has emerged most vigorously:

Brazil-focused South America; Mexico/U.S./Canada; Europe; and South and Southeast Asia. (The field is also growing vigorously in Africa, the Middle East, East Asia, and Australia/New Zealand, but these are much smaller clusters). All this, of course, has dramatically altered the field's élan and attractiveness. This is where the job growth is, not to mention the most challenging, value-rooted, and increasingly even well-paid jobs. Just listen to today's "business" school students.

Given the results-based power of this transformation of the citizen sector, more and more local changemakers are emerging. Some of these learn and later expand the pool of leading social entrepreneurs. To the degree they succeed locally, they give wings to the entrepreneur whose idea they have taken up, they encourage neighbors also to become changemakers, and they cumulatively build the institutions and attitudes that make local changemaking progressively easier and more respected. All of which eases the tasks facing the next generation of primary pattern-change entrepreneurs.

This virtuous cycle catalyzed by leading social entrepreneurs and local changemakers is the chief engine now moving the world toward an 'everyone a changemaker' future.

No matter how powerful this dynamic is, however, several other changes are necessary if society is to navigate this transition successfully:

Most important, society cannot significantly increase the proportion of adults who are, and know they are, changemakers and who have mastered the necessary and complex underlying social skills until it changes the way all young people live.

Although it is normal for support areas like finance to lag behind change in the operating areas they serve, the emergent citizen sector is now at significant risk unless it can quickly engineer major structural changes in both its institutional finance sector and the broad grassroots sources of support in its post-breakeven zone.

Transforming The Youth Years

The children of elite families grow up at home and usually in school, being expected to take initiative and being rewarded for doing so. This confident ability to master new situations and initiate whatever changes or actions are needed is in essence what defines the elite. Entering adult life with confidence and mastery of empathy/teamwork/leadership skills is what ultimately has given this small group control of the initiative and therefore of power and resources for millennia.

However, the other 97 percent grow up getting very little such experience with taking initiative. Adults control the classroom, work setting, and even sports and extra-curricular activities. And this situation, coupled with society's attitudes, drums home the message to this majority: "You're not competent or perhaps even responsible. Please don't try to start things; we can do it far better." Teachers, social workers and others are comfortably in control; and, in fact, most school and other youth cultures are not competent and do not train and support and respect initiative-taking. Instead, the peer group culture, not surprisingly, is resentful and in the worst cultures, quite negative.

Do these inarticulate, frustrated youth cultures bring analogous prior situations to mind? Over the last century, many other groups – including women, African Americans, those with disabilities, even colonial peoples – had to make their way from debilitating stereotypes and little prior practice in taking the initiative to becoming fully accepted, capable contributors. These groups, although very different from one another, had to travel strongly similar human and community transformation paths.

Young people are the last big group to set out on this journey. They are also different; but, in the underlying psychological and organizational transitions ahead, they can learn a great deal from the experience of these other groups.

Building on the history of these earlier movements and also on the accumulated experience of hundreds of leading social entrepreneurs working with young people, Ashoka and many partners have prototyped and are beginning to launch at scale the equivalent of a women's or older person's movement for young people.

Although this movement must ultimately change how everyone thinks about and relates to young people, it is young people and their peer communities who will have to change most and who have the most to gain. Therefore, as with all the earlier similar transformations, it is essential that they be central actors – both in actually shifting to the new pattern (because the best learning comes from action) and in championing the change (because people in any class are most likely to hear and trust peers).

Ashoka: Innovators for the Public

Ashoka is the global association of the world's leading social entrepreneurs – men and women with system-changing solutions that address the world's most urgent social challenges. Since its founding in 1980, Ashoka has launched and provided key long-term support to more than

1750 leading social entrepreneurs in over 60 countries. It provides these 'Ashoka Fellows' start-up stipends, professional services and a powerful global network of top social and business entrepreneurs. It also helps them spread their innovations globally.

Working with these social entrepreneurs, Ashoka builds communities of innovators who work together to transform society and design new ways for the citizen sector to become more entrepreneurial, productive and globally integrated. Ashoka's modest investments consistently yield extraordinary returns in every area of human need – from human rights to the environment, from economic development to youth empowerment. Five years after start-up launch, over 90 percent of Ashoka Fellows have seen independent institutions replicate their innovations, and over 50 percent have already changed national policy.

Muhammad Yunus, Nobel Peace Prize Winner 2006, has had significant collaboration with Ashoka Fellows as a founding member of Ashoka's Global Academy in 2001.

What is a Social Entrepreneur?

Social entrepreneurs are individuals with innovative solutions to society's most pressing social problems. They are ambitious and persistent, tackling major social issues and offering new ideas for wide-scale change.

Rather than leaving societal needs to the government or business sectors, social entrepreneurs find what is not working and solve the problem by changing the system, spreading the solution, and persuading entire societies to take new leaps.

Social entrepreneurs often seem to be possessed by their ideas, committing their lives to changing the direction of their field. They are both visionaries and ultimate realists, concerned with the practical implementation of their vision above all else.

Each social entrepreneur presents ideas that are user-friendly, understandable, ethical, and engage widespread support in order to maximize the number of local people who will stand up, seize their idea, and implement it. In other words, every leading social entrepreneur is a mass recruiter of local changemakers – a role model proving that citizens who channel their passion into action can do almost anything.

Over the past two decades, the citizen sector has discovered what the business sector learned long ago: there is nothing as powerful as a new idea in the hands of a first-class entrepreneur.

Why 'Social' Entrepreneur?

Just as entrepreneurs change the face of business, social entrepreneurs act as the change agents for society, seizing opportunities others miss and improving systems, inventing new approaches, and creating solutions to change society for the better. While a business entrepreneur might create entirely new industries, a social entrepreneur comes up with new solutions to social problems and then implements them on a large scale.

* Chapter is excerpted from *Kosmos* Journal – Fall | Winter 2007

Social Entrepreneurship –
Altering the Face of Business

Mirjam Schoening and Parag Gupta,
Schwab Foundation for Social Entrepreneurship

In the past few years social entrepreneurship has seen a meteoric rise in use that should be viewed with cautious triumph. A Lexis Nexis® search for social entrepreneur terms the year 2000, when the Schwab Foundation started, reveals only 264 stories. In the year of 2007, the same search yields 1,705 stories worldwide. Empirically, when the Schwab Foundation for Social Entrepreneurship invited its first social entrepreneur network members to the Annual Meeting or 'Davos' in 2002, it held an event entitled, "Meet the Social Entrepreneurs." It was dismally received with only a few participants in attendance – mainly to see the foundation's board members Paulo Coelho and Muhammad Yunus. Fast-forward eight years and social entrepreneurs are well regarded 'regulars' at Forum events. Indeed, workshops on building ventures with social entrepreneurs are some of the most acclaimed sessions at summits.

The Schwab Foundation for Social Entre-preneurship

The mission of the Schwab Foundation is to promote the notion of social entrepreneurship and the presence of social entrepreneurs on a global and regional level. It provides unparalleled platforms for the world's leadingsocial innovators at the regional and global levels that highlight social entrepreneurship as a key element to advance societies and address social problems in an innovative, sustainable and effective way.

The Foundation does not give grants, loans or make equity investments. Rather, it furthers the legitimacy of the work that social entrepreneurs do and facilitates unique partnerships with the corporate and public sectors that enable them to replicate and scale their groundbreaking efforts. The objectives of the Foundation are to

- identify and highlight the world's leading social entrepreneurs
- further provide legitimacy to their work
- provide access to usually inaccessible networks
- integrate social entrepreneurs in the relevant industry discussions with the key corporate players and prepare the ground for partnerships

As a sister affiliate to the World Economic Forum, the Foundation integrates world class social entrepreneurs into global programs at the Annual Meeting at Davos which gathers together corporate CEOs, heads of states, and civil society to improve the state of the world. The Foundation also works with the Forum on ongoing initiatives and expert councils to ensure innovative voices from grassroots practitioners are part of the dialogue. To ensure relevance, the Foundation focuses on the luminaries of the social entrepreneur world who have achieved national or international scale in their interventions.

To select these outstanding entrepreneurs, The Schwab Foundation works with media and corporate partners in 30 countries to search and select the "Social Entrepreneur of the Year" for the respective country. In addition, it receives nominations from third parties for social entrepreneurs not working in countries where the Foundation has still to establish country partnerships, or in countries where the social entrepreneur is not a citizen.

The three primary criteria for selection include:

1. **Innovation**: The candidate has brought about social change by transforming traditional practice. What is characteristic of a social entrepreneur is coming up with a pattern-changing idea and implementing it successfully.
2. **Direct positive social impact**: The candidate has developed and implemented the entrepreneurial initiative directly, together with poor or marginalised beneficiaries and stakeholders. Impact manifests itself in quantifiable results and testimonials and is well documented. There are no significant negative externalities. Intermediary organisations or foundations that seek to create social value through provision of financial and technical support to community-based groups will not be considered.
3. **Sustainability**: The candidate has generated the social conditions and/or institutions needed to sustain the initiative and is dedicating all of his/her time to it.

- If set up as a non-profit, the organization is achieving some degree of financial self-sustainability through fees or revenues or is engaged in creating mutually beneficial partnerships with business and/or the public sector. Where possible, economic incentives are embraced. In any case, there is a clear difference from traditional charity and a move towards community-based empowerment and sustainability. There is also a difference with traditional business.

- If set up as a for-profit, the orientation toward social and environmental value creation predominates, with financial return treated as a secondary means to an end, rather than an end in itself.

Other criteria taken into consideration include:

4. **Reach and Scope**: The social entrepreneur's initiative has spread beyond its initial context and has been adapted successfully to other settings in the country or internationally, either by the entrepreneur him or herself, or through others who have replicated or adapted elements of the initiative.
5. **Replicability**: The initiative can be adapted to other regions of the world to solve similar problems. It is scalable (can continue to grow and expand rapidly). The social entrepreneur is committed to openly sharing with others the tools, approaches and techniques that are critical to the adaptation of the initiative in different settings.

The candidate selected joins a community of the world's most accomplished entrepreneurs whose work focuses on public good creation – a community that learns from, and supports one another. Social entrepreneurs come together during the year at the regional meetings of the World Economic Forum in different parts of the world. The Foundation works with each social entrepreneur to provide every opportunity to showcase his/her innovative, market-based initiative that has proven to work to transform people's lives.

Professor Klaus Schwab created the World Economic Forum as an independent not-for-profit foundation in 1971 and built it into the foremost global partnership of business, political, intellectual and other leaders of society committed to improving the state of the world. In 1998, Klaus Schwab and his wife Hilde decided to create a second complementary foundation, the Schwab Foundation for Social Entrepre-neurship, with the purpose to promote social innovation. They stated: "… we want to find people who have discovered practical solutions to social problems at the local level, innovative solutions that have been shown to work to transform people's lives and that can be adapted to solve similar problems all around the world. I want to create a way to disseminate their accomplishments so others can support them or emulate their approaches."

As John Maynard Keynes noted that the greatest difficulty is not for people to accept new ideas, but to make them forget their old ideas.

Keynes sums up what we are trying to do. We are trying to change mindsets, stimulate the creation of new institutional arrangements to address the myriad of serious challenges and opportunities facing us today. To change the minds of leaders, we need to prove that another way IS possible, and that it is BEING DONE by change agents who have innovative ideas and practical solutions – social entrepreneurs. Changing those mindsets is a tough job. But it can be done. The core concept of capitalism has been economic gain through self-interest. While this has lead to economic freedom and prosperity, it has often come with unaccounted externalities like the environment and other public goods. Social entrepreneurs have started paving the path that does not make self-interest a zero-sum game but rather uses it as a tool towards mass empowerment and societal betterment.

What is Social Entrepreneurship?

To give a theoretical definition, it is about applying practical, innovative, market-based and sustainable approaches to benefit society in general, with an emphasis on the billions of people who fall through the cracks in every country around the world – whether those countries are industrialized or not. In sum, a social entrepreneur is able to take new ideas (sometimes innovating on existing ones), make them operational by applying business principles and, in the process, change mindsets and traditional practice, thus triggering systemic social change.

Simply put, a social entrepreneur equals one part Richard Branson and one part Mother Teresa mixed well.

The best way to understand social entrepreneurship is through examples of the social entrepreneurs themselves. As you will readily see, they have built their business models around sustainability rather than including sustainability as an afterthought. They are excellent examples for demonstrating how blended value actually is achieved and how sustainable social change can occur.

Iftekhar Enayetullah and Maqsood Sinha: 'One Man's Garbage...'

The first example is in Bangladesh where a financial bottom line meets a social and environmental bottom line. Two social entrepreneurs, Iftekhar Enayetullah and Maqsood Sinha – one an urban planner the other a civil engineer – teamed up to tackle the country's most pervasive environmental and health problems, starting with Dhaka, the capital. Every day in that city, 11 million people produce around 3,500 tons of solid waste, 80% of which is organic. The public waste collection service can only pick up half of that garbage and the rest is left to rot in the heat and humidity of the densely populated city, posing huge health problems.

Iftekhar and Maqsood, like entrepreneurs anywhere, saw an opportunity rather than a problem. They knew that in addition to the mounting garbage in the city, Bangladesh is facing excessive loss of topsoil fertility from overuse of chemical fertilizers and pesticides that also creep into rivers and canals and kill the fish. Both problems, the waste and the soil depletion, had a common solution.

Working in partnership with communities, Waste Concern has set in motion a process for house-to-house organic waste collection that is then taken to composting plants they have set up together with the communities. There, trained community members turn the waste into fertilizer. Waste Concern arranges for fertilizer companies and small nurseries to purchase and nationally market the compost-based bio-fertilizers it produces. The profits are invested to pay the slum dwellers that collect the waste and to continue to build expand the social enterprise. In addition, Waste Concern helps address Bangladesh's environmental problem of diminishing topsoil fertility by providing high quality compost.

By emphasizing the marketing aspect of organic waste and turning organic garbage into a "resource," Waste Concern has caused a chain reaction among multiple sectors in Bangladesh and has generated a socially transformational response to the problem of waste management.

They are now taking the company to the next phase. With the help of US$ 10 million investment from a waste treatment company in the Netherlands, Waste Concern has started capturing methane – a harmful greenhouse gas – from a landfill site in Dhaka and convert it into electricity that can be sold to local power utilities on a for-profit basis. They are pioneering international agreements between social sector organizations and international financing to 'template' carbon trading and build a robust carbon market between developing and developed nations. As the climate conversation ramps up worldwide and more environmentally friendly administrations on the horizon, visionary social entrepreneurs, like Iftekhar and Maqsood, will play an expanding role.

Waste Concern has demonstrated a profitable model to solve a public need – waste collection. Furthermore, their intervention not only provides local employment of marginalized communities, but also solves sanitary issues within the city, and benefits the environment.

David Green: Eye on Social Impact versus Profit

Waste Concern represents a commercially viable social and environmental enterprise. David Green, an American social entrepreneur, empowers marginalized citizens in developing countries by providing them needed goods and services and treating them as consumers.

David spent more than 15 years making expensive medical products affordable to the world's poorest people – and proving he can turn it into a sustainable, for-profit business. David's company, Catalytic Health, targets the huge untapped market of poor people in both industrialized and developing countries that established companies typically ignore because while potential sales volumes are huge, profit margins are slim. His company's overriding mission as a corporation is to demonstrate that it can use its core competency to serve first and foremost the base of the pyramid – to draw upon C.K. Prahalad's much quoted term for the mass market of poor consumers.

To illustrate, twelve years ago, he helped create Aurolab that is now one of the largest manufacturers in the world of intraocular lenses that eliminate cataracts, a leading cause of blindness. With sales of more than 600,000 units per year to 86 countries, Aurolab has 7.5% of the sector's global market share. And even though it sells its lenses for US$ 4 compared to over US$100 in the US, the company has profit margins of 52%. What makes Aurolab different from any other for-profit company? It cycles its profits back into the business, to further its social mission which is making high quality medical technology affordable and available to all.

What is this company's strategy? Its manufacturing costs are the same, if not more, than larger, more established companies. And it doesn't cut corners. It hires former heads of R&D from the best companies to design its products. The key components lie in the service delivery models and the fact that the company is looking to make money, but not maximize profits. For example, looking at the service delivery model that David implemented at Aravind Eye Care System (AECS) in India, the organization boasts the highest volume of eye surgery in the world. AECS regularly performs 250,000 eye operations, 80% were sight-restoring cataract surgeries. To achieve that volume, the hospital divides the entire workflow from intake to surgery and patient care into standardized procedures performed by super-specialists. Well-trained physicians perform as many as 50 surgeries a day. US hospitals do around four per week. And patients on average pay only US$ 50 per simple cataract operation whereas in the US the same procedure costs US$ 2,500. The efficiency allows the hospital to attain 52% profit margins, even though 65% of the care is provided free of charge or below costs.

David has also transformed funding flows to the social entrepreneurial space. With Deutsche Bank, he has created a $20 million eye fund that provides debt funding for the replication of Aravind Eye Care System's operation model to hospitals. This fund not only provides needed finance for hospitals to adopt the transformation and serve lower end patients but also provides a profitable investment in social markets that are traditionally associated with the grant - offering 100% commercial loss. David is now trying to replicate a similar process across other social sectors that can deliver a financial and social return.

Jose Ignacio Avalos: A Kilo of Food for Mal-nourished Children

The third example of social entrepreneurship is José Ignacio Avalos is one of the most prolific social entrepreneurs, having created more than 20 successful organizations.

Un Kilo de Ayuda (One Kilo of Help) was set up to fight malnutrition in children under 5 years of age with the vision to eradicate malnutrition entirely in Mexico by 2020. Under the program, carefully balanced food packages are distributed to more than 60,000 malnourished children in rural Mexico every two weeks. To determine the contents of the package, Un Kilo de Ayuda works with leading nutritionists in the world. But Avalos did not simply take the advice of the scientists, he relentlessly tested different compositions and delivery methods in the villages. They thus found out that the food package could not only be geared to the children. If the parents were hungry, they would eat first. The package now contains 12 products, half of them for the parents. The packages are not distributed for free, but at 50% of their value. While they are subsidized to make them affordable to the families, they are not distributed for free, as experience has shown that free gifts are not valued. Building in a market mechanism helps Un Kilo de Ayuda to gauge the attractiveness of its program.

Each child's weight and height gain, iron and vitamin A levels, are recorded and analyzed using the latest management information system. A severely malnourished child is, on average, fully recovered after 15 months, making Un Kilo de Ayuda the most successful malnutrition program in the world (the next one takes 24 months). Alleviating malnutrition in children younger than 5 years is one of the most effective ways of fighting poverty. Every dollar invested pays off with healthier children that are more capable of learning and more productive.

Un Kilo de Ayuda also runs three hospitals and clinics, treating around 100,000 patients a year. Before the hospitals were handed over to Un Kilo de Ayuda, they were 90% subsidized by grants. Un Kilo de Ayuda was able to make them operationally self-sufficient. The goal is to provide a replicable model for public and private entities, demonstrating that hospitals can cover their costs and still benefit the poorest population groups.

Jose Ignacio Avalos was also instrumental in setting up Compartamos, the fastest growing, largest and one of the most profitable microfinance institution in Latin America, which serves more than 800,000 clients. The organization has been a pioneer in proving not only that the poor are credit-worthy, but that the microfinance industry is investment-worthy. In April 2007, Compartamos was the first Latin American microfinance institution to offer equity through an Initial Public Offering (IPO). The shares were 13 times oversubscribed, valuing the bank at more than USD 1 billion – a hotly debated sensation in the microfinance field.

Avalos' latest program is Mi Tienda, a new kind of wholesaler that supplies small, rural shops with products at lower prices and in smaller quantities than traditional wholesalers. The idea for Mi Tienda sprung from the observation that the rural poor pay much higher prices for daily products at their local shops than urban populations with access to large discount stores. Mi Tienda delivers fresh products straight to the rural shops. These are able to offer a more varied and fresher inventory at lower prices. It also enables suppliers to get more of their goods into these markets with faster turnover. Indirectly, Mi Tienda ensures the long term success of Un Kilo's nutrition programs.

'Doing So' When Others Say 'No'

Interesting enough, in these cases, business and government have to be goaded into action. Like most true social entrepreneurs, David, Iftekhar, Maqsood, and José Ignacio wanted to first and foremost solve a prescient problem – be it a commonly afflictive eye condition, heaping piles of waste, or malnutrition. Perseverance in their endeavors, like in commercial ventures, was critical. In Avalos' case, his first iteration of the venture was handing out scientifically developed food packages. Through relentless measurements, Avalos found out that this method did not have the desired impact and developed a better suited package in endless reiterations with the mothers and the scientists. Avalos was persistent and soon developed an intervention to deal with this root cause.

A difference from the commercial sector in these cases however, is that the social entrepreneurs were open with their innovation and indeed were happy to provide their innovative new methods to existing players within their market rather than hoard them. In David's case, he went to many pharmaceutical/biotechnology firms with his concept of a down-market Inter Ocular Lens. They all scoffed wanting demonstrated success. Iftekhar and Maqsood sought to convince government agencies to develop the community-based composting plants, even promising free consulting services to support public sector efforts. But they could not convince the authorities. One government official listened to their ideas and then challenged them: if their ideas for community-managed compost plants were so great, why didn't they create it themselves?

This is illustrative of two key traits of entrepreneurs. First, the drive to innovate where none dare tread and second, to do rather than postulate. Bill Gates is often credited for saying, "If you can show me the business plan, it is already too late." Social entrepreneurs are mavericks. People like stability and shun change. Mavericks who seek to disrupt the established order of things are not welcome. Most managers and civil servants deal with what is. Entrepreneurs focus on creating things the world has never seen. Yet the world does not give entrepreneurs sufficient status or opportunity to transform societies for the better. Originality and creativity are still viewed with suspicion.

Just look at employment policies in most government or corporate institutions. When reviewing candidates, invariably they look for evidence of academic achievement and a boring steadiness that produces good exam pass rates and grades rather than for experiences that might suggest that a candidate is innovative and inspired, perhaps even rebellious. This is because most organizations have a low tolerance for mistakes. Risk-averse societies and organizations keep people from failing. They also keep them from trying. Attitudes towards setbacks and failure are a major factor in nurturing or curtailing the spirit of innovation and invention. Thomas Edison captures this attitude brilliantly (excuse the pun) when he quipped, "I have not failed. I have found 10,000 ways it won't work."

Secondly, entrepreneurs take action and are spurred by societal inertia. Telling an entrepreneur, "It can't be done" is tantamount to waving a bright red cape in front of a bull. David Green built his prototype and took it to developing markets. When the government told the 'Garbage Brothers' to do it themselves, they did. They founded Waste Concern.

The social aspect comes through in the above examples as the social entrepreneurs undertake both public and private sector functions simultaneously. On the one hand, they work with those populations that governments have been unable to reach effectively or have ignored. On the other, they address market failures by providing access to private goods and services where business does not operate - because the risks are too great and the financial rewards too few. With little market rewards or assistance, social entrepreneurs are reshaping the architecture for building sustainable and peaceful societies.

Collaboration and the Shifting Role of Businesses

There is no doubt that the modern corporation as we know it today has empowered individual genius and bestowed great social benefits. Yet it has also done social harm. Many of the ills of modern life – nonsustainable levels of personal and institutional debt, toxic air and water, workplace injury, loss of livelihoods for communities, political bribery – can be traced to a corporate lack of responsibility. This is not intentional. No one wants to cause poverty, pollution, disease, unemployment and corruption. Rather, they want to make profits. But in that pursuit, externalities slip through the cracks. To achieve profits in the short term, corporations exact a "social and environmental price" and that price is high and rising. Up until recently, a segment of society was trying to maximize profits without concern for the impact on the well being of the society as a whole, while another segment of social organizations would have to deal with the fall out. This is now changing as the lines between 'civil society' and business blur and transcend former boundaries as demonstrated by our examples above. Our first example, Waste Concern, operates in a space *The New York Times* recently referred to as the 'fourth sector' –organizations driven by both social purpose and financial promise that fall somewhere between traditional companies and charities. These hybrid organizations come from the social sector angle looking for a more self-sustaining model to the commercial angle with corporations understanding consumer demands for more environmental or socially conscious products. It spans the gamut of 'market caps' from small footwear companies to General Electric's Ecomagination campaign; from local restaurants to Toyota's hybrid cars. These companies have transcended the short term glitz of Corporate Social Responsibility and evolved to Corporate Social Opportunity – where social benefit is embedded in the business as directly contributing to the financial mission rather than a side marketing gimmick. This movement is the yang to the yin of social entrepreneurship. In the case of Un Kilo de Ayuda, the corporate partners gain valuable insight into lower-income markets. Social entrepreneurs, obsessed with scale, in return gain from these partnerships which help to expand impact in ways previously not possible.

Finally, in the case of David Green and Aurolab, we see how social entrepreneurs act as 'bleeding edge' innovators that can lead even the world's largest and most profitable companies in figuring out how to access new markets and build their brand as responsible companies. As social entrepreneurs place social impact above commercial profit, their trial and error and innovation helps lead the way towards sustainable and profitably viable methods of serving base of pyramid customers. This will be critical in coming years as the Base of Pyramid – or the three to four billion currently untapped by capital markets – represents a five trillion dollar market that is ever increasing.

The Role of Government and Social Entrepreneurship

Governments, also, have much to gain from supporting social entrepreneurs. But they should not make the mistake of seeing them as simple service delivery subcontractors. Social entrepreneurs are system's changers. Like business entrepreneurs who are the innovators in the corporate sector, social entrepreneurs are the innovators of the public sector. Governments should heed regulatory and policy changes necessary to foster social impact. Social entrepreneurs, as trail blazers, usually provide an early indication of the forthcoming needs of society. For example, in India, fraudulent behavior in the banking sector had caused the government to severely regulate the ability of financial institutions to set up savings accounts for their clients. However now, this same law has set a high hurdle for microfinance institution to start a savings account for their clients/beneficiaries so they may break out from the cycle of poverty. There are many other examples all over the world of such policies that hamper the sector work of various social entrepreneurs.

However, social entrepreneurship is becoming an increasingly recognized term even among government circles. In the United States, President Barack Obama, during his Presidential Election campaign has proposed to create a Social Entrepreneur Agency to support socially innovative projects in the same manner the government supports small businesses. In addition, Obama has called for a Social Investment Fund Network to also provide financial backing. Similarly, governments in general must find the best manner by which to create the needed support systems to allow them to innovate and scale, without wanting to take over the innovation process and kill it as a result.

Paving the Way for Change

In conclusion, social entrepreneurs show us how to uphold social and environmental goals without eschewing financial sustainability. They remind us that balance between those three goals can be achieved and pioneer bleeding edge practices of how to do so – paving the way for systems change. We at the Schwab Foundation believe this is a critical moment in history for social entrepreneurship. The last century was characterized by the triumph of market economics. Business entrepreneurs made millions and shaped the aspirations of a worldwide public who dreamed of emulating them. But the wealth generated benefited primarily educated and skilled populations. Capitalism was unable to bring the majority of the world's population. Most countries have realized the downsides of the economic model, and so they are caught in a dilemma of how to implement a model that promises strong economic growth – but needs a social vision that incorporates their poor millions into the system and its benefits.

And this is where social entrepreneurs can help along the way. They recognize that the problems of economic and social inequality are too complex to be left only to the corporate, the public or the charitable sectors. They know that the problems we currently face have arisen precisely because of a dichotomized world – where the spheres that generate financial wealth are separated from the spheres where public policy and programs are framed. To redress that situation, social entrepreneurs create innovative, hybrid organizations that look like businesses – indeed, they may be set up as for-profit organizations, but their bottom line is social value creation. Social entrepreneurs are revolutionaries – but too practical to be of the placard-carrying type.

But they cannot change the world in isolation. Their efforts need to be closely intertwined with the public and corporate sector as well as with the rest of civil society. Their role is to ignite the fire of social transformation. This is not business as usual. That flame must be fanned and nurtured by those who understand what social entrepreneurship is about and delight in its promise for what it can achieve – with the help of all of us.

Entrepreneurial Solutions to Insoluble Problems

John Elkington and Pamela Hartigan,
Volans Ventures

It is clear that the world faces epochal challenges – from outright conflict, terrorism, and weapons of mass destruction; to poverty and hunger; to the threat of global pandemics and, perhaps the biggest issue of all, climate change. But, tackled in the right way, today's crises will lead to tomorrow's solutions, and the size of the potential market opportunities is staggering.

There are an estimated 4 billion low-income consumers, constituting a majority of the world's population, and they make up what is called the "base of the (economic) pyramid," or BOP. An ever-expanding body of research is exploring how to use market-based approaches to "better meet their needs, increase their productivity and incomes, and empower their entry into the formal economy." BOP markets are far from small: it is estimated, for example, that the BOP market in Asia (including the Middle East) is made up of 2.86 billion people with a total income of $3.47 trillion. In Eastern Europe it is estimated at $458 billion; in Latin America, $509 billion; and in Africa, $429 billion. In total, these markets are thought to be worth some $5 trillion.

But how can mainstream business, financial, and political leaders best come to grips with these emerging trends in value creation? Three answers immediately spring to mind. First, they can experiment with new business models, as much of the BOP literature suggests. Second, as leading business thinkers have long argued, a can-do attitude is much more likely to succeed than don't-do, won't-do, or can't-do mind-sets. And, third, it makes sense to track down, study, and work alongside can-do and we-can-work-out-how-to-do-it innovators and entrepreneurs who are already hard at work on developing real-world solutions. That is what we have been doing since the turn of the millennium – identifying, studying, networking, and supporting some of the world's most successful social and environmental entrepreneurs. The results can be found in our new book, *The Power of Unreasonable People*[1].

But, first, a word or two about the book's title. "The reasonable man adapts himself to the world," playwright George Bernard Shaw once said, whereas "the unreasonable one persists in trying to adapt the world to himself. Therefore all progress depends on the unreasonable man." By this definition, not only are most of the entrepreneurs described in the following pages unreasonable – many have actually been dubbed "crazy," even by family and friends – but a large slice of the future may hinge on their success in spreading their apparently unhinged ideas and business models.

So where can such changes and change agents be found? Time and again during periods of extraordinary volatility, disruption, and change, the best place to look for clues to tomorrow's revolutionary business models is at the fringes of the current dysfunctional system, so that's where we headed. The journey has taken us from the mainstream to the margins – from the Alpine meetings of the global elite in Davos and gatherings of social entrepreneurs in places like São Paulo to the festering waste dumps of Bangladesh; from top business schools to violence-torn countries in the Middle East and HIV-plagued communities across Africa. In the process, we believe that we have found clues to the ways in which all businesses – large or small, corporate or entrepreneurial – will operate in tomorrow's markets.

Whistle-Stop Survey Of The World

So where can we find social entrepreneurs? The answer is everywhere, although certain countries and regions tend to turn up more than their fair share. When, a few years ago, we analyzed the list of Schwab Foundation entrepreneurs, a rough head count showed the continents falling into the following sequence, from the most entrepreneurs to the least:

The greatest concentration of Asian social entrepreneurs is found in the Indian subcontinent. Three countries of the four in the region – India, Pakistan, and Bangladesh – are well represented. There are many reasons for this high level of activity, including the political problems that the region has suffered since its partition in the 1940s, the sheer scale of the poverty-related dilemmas that have dogged these countries, and the extraordinary number of natural disasters that have affected them – including the tsunami of late 2004.

Next stop, Latin America. Again, there are many reasons why social entrepreneurship has taken root in the region. Apart from population pressures, widespread poverty, and growing environmental problems, governments there have historically been weak, corrupt, and ineffective. To try to fill the vacuum, many of the churches in these countries have encouraged entrepreneurial solutions to social problems. If you run down the Schwab Foundation's worldwide list of outstanding entrepreneurs, the largest number from any single country outside the United States (with twenty) comes from Brazil (with nine).

It may seem surprising, given the economic wealth of North America overall, to learn that the United States had the most number of social entrepreneurs in the Schwab Foundation listing, but the facts speak for themselves. You find such entrepreneurs everywhere in the United States, from the high-tech world of Silicon Valley to the many Native American reservations and their sometimes Third World living conditions. An example of the latter is the First Nations Development Institute, founded by Rebecca Adamson, a Cherokee, which has spearheaded a cultural paradigm shift in Native American communities, encouraging entrepreneurship instead of passivity. It's true that many American social entrepreneurs target the rest of the world's problems, but a surprising number are also focusing on homegrown issues. They include people working to support the growing numbers of elderly as well as those fighting to protect the interests of independent workers, from nannies and taxi drivers to software designers and consultants.

So what makes some countries and regions more successful in spawning social entrepreneurs? It is a combination of major challenges (as in the Indian subcontinent), relatively weak governments (though the United Kingdom and the United States are exceptions), a culture that encourages or at least doesn't stall entrepreneurship, and favorable legal and tax regimes. Over time, we expect countries around the world to become much more focused on developing the conditions that encourage and support these unreasonable people, these market-creating social and environmental entrepreneurs.

New Wave of Creative Destruction

The world is moving into a new era of creative destruction, as the economist Joseph Schumpeter described the processes of economic degeneration and regeneration[2]. The old caterpillar economic models are beginning to morph into more sustainable variants, but the process is likely to be at least as painful and protracted as the changes that marked the period between the two World Wars[3]. In the process, profound new challenges are opening up for business decision-makers, financial investors and public policy-makers. Incumbent companies are struggling to respond effectively to the new order, opening out enormous opportunity spaces for new types of entrepreneurs. Corporate strategies are beginning to shift from their 1.0 variants (focused on compliance) and 2.0 successors (that increasingly have emphasised corporate citizenship) to much more powerful 3.0 thinking (which focuses on creating the new markets that will drive more sustainable forms of development).

This latest wave of change will spotlight the capacity of leading companies not only to respond to such changes but also to help drive them. Still, the scale of the relevant challenges continues to outrun our collective capacity to deliver. That gap will eventually be closed—the key question is by whom and at what cost? Entrepreneurs – both in the private and public sectors – will play central roles.

Of course, entrepreneurship has been enjoying a pretty extended honeymoon period, stretching back – in the latest cycle – at least to the days of Margaret Thatcher and Ronald Reagan. Although periodic onsets of irrational exuberance have inevitably tarnished some entrepreneurial halos, both the public and private sectors continue to call for better environments to promote the deployment of entrepreneurial solutions. And into this landscape a new set of entrepreneurs is erupting, focusing on a wide range of social and environmental challenges that some people cluster under the heading of sustainable development.

This process is being accelerated as a growing array of socio-economic, environmental and governance dilemmas press in on mainstream decision-makers. These include challenges such as climate change, the risk of global pandemics, the growing threat to natural resources like water and fisheries, and the ever-present issues of poverty, hunger and disease[4]. At a time when such prospects seem to narrow and darken our horizons, talented entrepreneurs are creating a wealth of new opportunities. For all of us to benefit into the long run, we must ensure real opportunity for a much, much greater proportion of the global population. Recent work by SustainAbility and Volans Ventures attempts to assess the current state of social and environmental, entrepreneurship. While an over-emphasis on definitions can be distracting, general working explanations of the terms can help us better identify these pioneers.

Social entrepreneurs are entrepreneurs whose new ventures (social enterprises) prioritize social returns on investment. These people aspire to achieve higher leverage than conventional philanthropy and NGOs, often aiming to transform the systems whose dysfunctions help create or aggravate major socioeconomic, environmental, and political problems.

By contrast, environmental entrepreneurs may be interested in social objectives, but their main focus is environmental. Some commentators consider environmental entrepreneurship to be a subset of social entrepreneurship, but they are distinct. A major rebranding of the environmental technology sector began in 2002, as the 'cleantech' sector. The Cleantech Venture Network (CVN) defines cleantech as embracing a diverse range of products, services, and processes that are inherently designed to provide superior performance at lower costs, greatly reduce or eliminate environmental impacts and, in doing so, improve the quality of life. CVN includes the following sectors: energy generation; energy storage; energy infrastructure; energy efficiency; transportation & logistics; water purification & management; air quality; materials & nanotechnology; manufacturing/industrial; agriculture & nutrition; materials recovery and recycling; environmental IT and enabling technologies.

Both social and environmental entrepreneurship address market failures, though the former tends to address failures that are endemic and deep-seated, while the latter increasingly targets opportunities that are closer to market. Strikingly, after a decades-long period of adaptation, at least some of our great environmental challenges are now seen as potentially soluble through the use of new business models and technologies. Our focus is on the possibilities presented by the new societal mindsets, the hurdles entrepreneurs face in scaling their organizations and the opportunities for greater collaboration with mainstream corporations, government and others.

Powerful Catalyst for Change

Social entrepreneurship is emerging as a powerful catalyst of the sort of change that governments and business are increasingly committed to – but rarely know how to deliver. And through these new firms, the potential for holistic breakthrough solutions is considerable – and growing. Among the routes to scale discussed by our respondents, the following surfaced repeatedly: (1) grow individual social enterprises; (2) establish multiple enterprises; (3) get big organizations – whether companies, public agencies or NGOs – to adopt the relevant models and approaches; and (4) spur public policy legislation designed to fix market failures.

Although to keep us grounded, we should point out that while the field may be growing, it remains relatively small. To put rough numbers on the three areas of social enterprise, cleantech and philanthropy, we estimate that less than $200 million is going into social enterprise worldwide from dedicated foundations each year, compared to over $2 billion into cleantech in the USA and EU and well over $200 billion into philanthropy in the USA alone.

Even with these impressive numbers, money remains the main headache. Accessing capital is the No. 1 challenge for the entrepreneurs we surveyed, with almost three-quarters (72%) putting this at the top of their priority list. Foundations are still the favorite source of funding for social entrepreneurs (mentioned by 74% of respondents), but there is a wide recognition of the need to diversify funding sources. Turning this goal into an action plan, many entrepreneurs believe this financial self-sufficiency is a real prospect within five years. The proportion of respondents expecting to be funding their own operations over the same timescale, with little or no dependence on grants, jumped from 8% currently to 28%.

With the need for new funding, there is a real appetite to partner with business. Social and cleantech entrepreneurs are equally interested in developing partnerships with business – but with different expectations. Social entrepreneurs, in particular, are acutely aware that they often lack the experience and skills needed. A constant refrain was the growing need for brokering between the entrepreneurs and potential business partners.

Locking into a particular view of entrepreneurship could cause us to miss the breadth of effort. For example, it's easy to get excited about small start-ups in the renewable energy field, but we should remember the huge contributions already being made by much larger companies like Acciona based in Spain, Vestas in Denmark or GE in the USA. And there is also a need to focus on ways of supporting social intrapreneurs, the change agents working inside major corporations and financial institutions.

But, business can only go so far alone, for real system change we must focus on government. Governments need to do more to shape public policy, public sector targets and wider incentives – for example in relation to tax breaks for the funding of social enterprise.

Fields on a roll tend to become less exciting over time and interest can shift elsewhere. However, the growing importance of the challenges these entrepreneurs are trying to address guarantees that even if there are upturns and downturns in their fortunes, the underlying growth trajectory will be strongly upward. Their clear interest in working with mainstream business and financial institutions distinguishes them sharply from many conventional NGOs – and their capacity to create and deliver real-world solutions makes them significantly more interesting to business. On the government front, a fair proportion of the leading social entrepreneurs have already worked to shape public policy to favour and support their new approaches, with varying degrees of success.

Growing Interest in Entrepreneurship

Wherever we look, we see growing interest among business leaders in what social entrepreneurs are doing. Several factors seem to be central in driving this trend. They also contribute to the blurring of the responsibilities between public and private realms.

First, twenty years after the Brundtland Commission first put sustainable development onto the political agenda[5], a number of major challenges once seen to be (and often dismissed as) the preserve of activist NGOs and wider civil society have pushed forcefully into the political and business mainstream. This process is often reinforced by the withdrawal or weakening of government activity. Successive summit meetings of the World Economic Forum, for example, have focused on an increasingly interconnected agenda linking such issues as poverty, hunger, pandemic risks, terrorism, human rights, energy security, and the growing threat of climate destabilization.

Second, despite the huge progress achieved in corporate citizenship and corporate social responsibility over the past 10-15 years, there is a growing concern that we may be reaching the "limits of CSR." The *Harvard Business Review*[6] neatly captured this mood with a twinned pair of articles by Michael Porter and Mark Kramer ('Strategy and Society: The Link Between Competitive Advantage and Corporate Social Responsibility') and Clayton Christensen ('Disruptive Innovation for Social Change'). The conclusion: too many companies have seen the new, interconnected agenda as remote from their core business interests. The reality is that these complex issues pose increasingly strategic choices that need to be addressed in suitably radical and higher leverage ways – something that most corporate citizenship departments seem ill-equipped to do. But the pressures are clear, as in Wal-Mart's announcement that it will impose new climate footprint specifications and requirements on its 61,000 suppliers. This is one more indication that changes can come from private sector initiative far faster than when government and public policy channels are attempted and, often, blocked by effective corporate lobbying.

Third, a number of major corporations have begun to rebundle existing activities – and in some cases launch new ones – designed to meet sustainability-related needs. A case in point has been GE, with its 'ecomagination' initiative[7]. To illustrate the scale at which such companies can drive change, if minded to do so: when GE released its 2006 ecomagination report, it revealed that revenues from the sale of energy efficient and environmentally advanced products and services had doubled from $6 billion to $12 billion, with orders in the pipeline jumping from $17 billion to $50 billion. The key point here is that markets are changing and that new offerings are going to be urgently required. Companies that unleash the talents of their intrapreneurs – and form alliances with leading external social and environmental entrepreneurs – will be better placed to succeed.

Fourth, we have seen the emergence of two separate movements that have helped push entrepreneurial solutions further into the spotlight. (1) The social enterprise sector has been building for decades, but has been given a major boost by the work of Ashoka and initiatives launched by The Schwab Foundation, The Skoll Foundation, Acumen, Endeavor and Fast Company (particularly its Social Capitalist Awards) and many others across the world. (2) The 'cleantech' sector, in part a rebranding of environmental and energy-related enterprise, has seen rapid growth thanks to growing concerns around energy security and climate change – and the recent shift at least in the rhetoric of leading U.S. politicians around issues like climate change[8].

Time to Think Different

To have any chance of changing the world, entrepreneurial solutions must offer relatively high leverage, replicability and scale, and – fundamentally – become part of the market mainstream. Pretty much without exception, the social entrepreneurs we have interviewed are supportive of the idea of partnerships with corporations. They are interested to further develop those partnerships they already had, and to build new ones. This potentially transforms the landscape, shifting the debate from the old, forced choice between giant companies (that struggle to connect and act) or much smaller niche companies (that struggle to reach meaningful scale). In the process, the rise of very different forms of business-to-business and peer-to-peer cooperation holds out real promise of advancing our collective response to very different levels.

The business case for corporate responsibility and sustainability is ever evolving, but always pertinent. The biggest reason that business needs to engage is, bluntly, that the world is changing – and with it markets. Social and environmental entrepreneurs do not have all the answers, but they do see the world and markets differently, and the more innovative are experimenting with new business models that could potentially break out of their niches and help transform key elements of the global economy.

Just as software morphs through successive generations, 1.0, 2.0 and so on, we conclude that the time has come for what we call 3.0 thinking in relation to sustainability challenges. If 1.0 was driven by regulators and promoted a compliance mindset in business, 2.0 has been more about corporate citizenship, based on transparency, accountability and a growing array of voluntary initiatives. By contrast, 3.0 thinking, strategy and ventures are different, in that, this wave seeks transformative market and sustainability outcomes[9]. It is about creative destruction, as Joseph Schumpeter called it, and about creative reconstruction.

In essence, Mindset 3.0 is about seeing, or 're-perceiving'[10], immense challenges. For example, with the growing risk of abrupt climate change comes potential opportunities to leverage the power of markets and business to reboot entire economic and political systems. This is exactly what is beginning to happen in the energy field. In some cases the time-scales involved may be generational, but the transformation is clearly under way. While the cleantech landscape is now largely populated with pure-play profit seekers, the industry was pioneered by individuals who saw the opportunity to leverage market drivers, such as energy security, stability and cost, to realize significant environmental outcomes.

There are a multitude of potential benefits to any company partner working with high performance social and environmental entrepreneurs. Among them is the outsourcing of risk. By outsourcing research into sensitive or unfamiliar areas, such as pharmaceuticals for emerging markets, new energy alternatives, or enhanced foods, companies can minimize potential brand risks, while remaining close to emerging trends. They also may be able to bypass strict internal controls around return on investment criteria that would prevent the company investing internally in high risk, entrepreneurial ventures.

Social and environmental business partnerships can provide access to information, markets and networks. Many social entrepreneurs are working with populations, and in communities, unfamiliar to large corporations. It's true people like Vandana Shiva would no doubt shudder at the idea of opening up wider links between corporations and such grassroots ventures and for good reason, and we should remain acutely nervous about such initiatives being driven in the interests of companies like Coca-Cola or Nestlé. However, with the right caution and balance, the scaling and effective replication of successful solutions can dramatically gain from the resources of the big battalions. The key challenge here will be to select corporate partners strategically, and then to manage the resulting partnerships to hold them true to the small organization's founding values.

The interests of the potential partners often coincide in various ways. Many entrepreneurs have an interest in helping build markets for affordable and accessible mainstream products, for example. On the corporate side, collaboration offers companies access to information about potential consumers and partners and in many cases, lends additional credibility. It can also spread inspiration. Collaboration with social and environmental entrepreneurs can help companies to tap and recharge their own entrepreneurial and creative spirits, resulting in innovative new product development (e.g. microinsurance, 'green' products). Consumer goods companies, such as Nike and Marks & Spencer, are beginning to look to social entrepreneurs as a source of originality and competitive advantage for turning out new products.

Potential for Revolutionary Change

Those who have worked in this field for some time are excited by the pace of developments at the interface between business and social enterprise. "The sleeping giant is awakening," says Sara Olsen of Social Venture Technology Group. "The potential for cross fertilization between social enterprise and mainstream corporations is huge – it's utterly revolutionary[11]!" All true, but for all of this to survive and thrive, the new mindsets, the new business models and the new technologies and tools will have to find traction in markets as they are today. Over time, as the entrepreneurs learn how to work with the more thoughtful big companies, they can begin to lobby more effectively for governments to shape markets to favour these new approaches.

Clearly, all of this needs to come with a powerful public health warning. While our survey revealed willingness on the part of social entrepreneurs to engage corporations, it also highlighted concerns about the potential for mission creep, brand erosion and power imbalances. The implications of these impending shifts are substantial for the NGOs who have done most of the work to date, for companies that have begun to adapt their operations to the relevant challenges in compliance and citizenship, for the entrepreneurs who will need to work out how to deliver across the value spectrum, and for public policymakers who will need to work out how to shape markets towards more sustainable, more just outcomes.

Feedback from the more seasoned entrepreneurs in our sample offered insights into what would make some of these new partnerships work. A number of them echoed the advice of more traditional NGOs[12], noting that partnerships work best when there is a clear set of principles and expectations guiding the partnership (e.g., we only work on projects related to our mission, we respect commercial confidentiality, we understand our business partner's need to pursue ventures that allow them to make a profit). They also stressed that the entrepreneur and partner must have comparable levels of interest in the partnership.

Longer term partnerships are typically preferred, with social entrepreneurs seeing their organizations and the environments in which they operate as complex, requiring time for an outsider to learn. Cleantech companies, in particular, want to bring in corporate partners early to ensure later options for potential acquisition, what they describe as a "locked-in exit strategy."

The role of internal champions in partner companies is cited as essential to building good partnerships. For Gary Hirshberg of Stonyfield Farm, when being acquired by Danone, this was the French food company's CEO, Franck Riboud. Clearly, however, this approach poses real dangers when the individual moves or leaves. Even with engagements that occur at the senior management/corporate level, there are concerns about partners pulling out, indicating a need for entrepreneurs to be adaptable, have a Plan B, and avoid relying on any one individual or department for support.

Overall, our conclusion is that the optimism about these new entrepreneurs is well placed, but that they are experiencing a range of growing pains – and there is an urgent need to steer more capital and business resources into this area. If this can be achieved, we very much agree with Tim Freundlich (Director, Strategic Initiatives, Calvert Social Investment Foundation[13] and Founding Principal, Good Capital[14]) that the outlook is bright. "I see the social enterprise landscape rapidly prototyping strategies that corporations will incorporate; replicate – or just plain steal. These entrepreneurs act as fearless and fast actualizers, taking the uncertainty and lack of imagination out of the equation for mainstream business."

Business 3.0 will be business as unusual, as the late social entrepreneur Anita Roddick put it, and it will involve a radical new set of natural selection processes operating upon value chains, business models, companies, industry sectors and, in the ultimate analysis, entire economies. But at the end of this historic reordering of value creation we will have found solutions that address many – though certainly not all – of the great social and environmental problems that today seem to be impenetrable.

Notes

1. John Elkington and Pamela Hartigan, *The Power of Unreasonable People: How Social Entrepreneurs Create Markets That Change the World*, Harvard Business Press, 2008
2. Thomas K. McCraw, Prophet of Innovation: *Joseph Schumpeter and Creative Destruction*, Harvard University Press, 2007
3. See, for example, John Elkington, *The Chrysalis Economy, How Citizen CEOs and Corporations Can Fuse Values and Value Creation*, Capstone/John Wiley, 2001
4. SustainAbility, *Growing Opportunity: Entrepreneurial Solutions to Insoluble Problems*, with Allianz, DuPont and The Skoll Foundation, 2007.
5. *Our Common Future*, Report of the World Commission on Environment and Development ('Brundtland Commission'), Oxford University Press, 1987
6. See *Harvard Business Review*, December 2006
7. http://ge.ecomagination.com/@v=022120072196@/site/index.html
8. One of the most notable actors in this sector is the Cleantech Venture Network, http://www.cleantech.com
9. Mindset 1.0 has tended to be driven by necessity and by the pressure to comply with emerging regulations and rules. Mindset 2.0 approaches include enhanced stakeholder engagement, sustainability reporting and cause-related marketing, but typically do not offer the prospect of systemic transformation. By connecting to a company's core business, Mindset 3.0 shifts responses into a different gear.
10. For more, see the work of scenario planners Pierre Wack and Peter Schwartz.
11. The results of a study by Sara Olsen and Paul Herman on the environmental and social performance of 21 main stream corporations were published in *Fast Company*, April 2007.
12. See *The 21st Century NGO: In the Market for Change*, SustainAbility, The UN Global Compact and United Nations Environment Programme, 2003
13. http://www.calvertfoundation.org/
14. http://www.goodcap.net

Be Bold – A Movement Begins with an Idea*

Lara Galinsky, Echoing Green

Taking on the World

The social problems of our time – such as poverty, hunger, home-lessness, and educational inequities – are complex and deeply rooted. Many people turn away because these problems are too overwhelming, painful, or removed from their daily lives. Some people, responding to faith, family, or their own moments of obligation, choose to get involved and make a difference.

Doing charitable work through volunteerism and public service, donating money and resources, or working in the nonprofit sector are key ways to ease the suffering of the less fortunate. On the other hand, working for social change requires you to be bold and to envision big solutions to big social problems.

Bold thinkers have the gall to challenge the status quo and ask the really hard questions: Why should one citizen matter less than another? What stands in the way of equal opportunity for all? Why shouldn't the wealth of a society be measured by its service and commitment to others? These thinkers have the gall to dismiss the limitations society can place on those with new and different ideas. They transcend the limitations they place on themselves and their dreams because they believe they can take on the world and make a real impact. Quite simply, they have the gall to think big.

Those with the gall to think big are "practical idealists." Their idealism is boundless and constant – a North Star that carries them through doubt and challenges. Their confidence and ability to self-affirm help them press for the change they wish to see in the world. Yet they do not dismiss reality or insist on an unrelentingly positive view of the world.

With hard work and the willingness to learn from their mistakes, these audacious thinkers learn how to execute their visions and bring a high level of strategic thinking to their ideas and organizations. This makes them effective as well as visionary leaders.

A Movement Begins with an Idea

Wendy Kopp grew up in a comfortable neighborhood in Dallas, Texas. The public high school she attended, which was comparable to a top private school, spent ample resources on infrastructure, athletics, and other extracurricular activities. It was assumed that Wendy, like most of her classmates, would graduate and attend college. In the fall of 1984, Wendy matriculated at Princeton University.

Wendy's interest in educational policy was sparked during her first weeks at Princeton as she watched her freshman-year roommate, a gifted poet, struggle with her coursework. Wendy's roommate told her about attending public high school in challenging circumstances in the South Bronx, New York. Wendy was troubled by the inequality between her educational experience and her roommate's; she knew that her high-school education gave her a significant advantage at Princeton.

As a public policy major, Wendy studied this country's educational system. After deciding to make real what she was only reading about in books, she organized a conference that connected students with business leaders to discuss the nation's education problems. Rising student enrollment and an impending surge in teacher retirement meant that the United States was headed toward a decade of teacher shortages. Poor rural areas and big cities were already feeling these shortages, and student performance was suffering as a result. In urban and rural areas, an elementary-school child worked at a level three grades behind his or her counterpart in wealthier suburbs. And a child born into urban communities, such as the Bronx or Compton, was seven times less likely to graduate from college than a child born in Manhattan or Beverly Hills. During one session of the conference, many students expressed interest in teaching at public schools as a way of combating these educational inequities.

With the conference over and the graduation looming, Wendy began looking for a job. But nothing struck her as the right fit. Many of her friends were also struggling to find the right careers. Investment banks and consulting firms recruited aggressively on campus. Some students accepted two-year positions at these companies in the hopes that they would learn a lot and then pursue more public-service careers. Other graduating seniors, including Wendy, looked for a direct pathway to service immediately after graduation.

Wendy was required to write a senior thesis in order to graduate. Sensing an opportunity, she began pulling together the many threads of her personal and educational experiences. She decided that bright college graduates who were searching for meaningful, challenging careers might find fulfillment by working in underserved schools. Wendy envisioned an initiative in which new college graduates would be recruited for teaching jobs just as they were recruited for positions in investment banking and consulting. The talent and energy of these new graduated could bet he perfect solution to an enduring problem. As teachers, recent graduates could have an immense impact on the lives of disadvantaged children. In turn, the teaching experience would help shape the recruits' lifelong career paths and affirm their civic commitment.

Wendy's thesis became the blueprint for her new idea, which she called **Teach For America**. Wendy's detailed business plan relied on her gall to think big. She proposed a first-year budget of $2.5 million and an initial corps of 500 teachers, talented recent college graduates who would commit to teaching two years in both urban and rural underserved schools across the United States. Wendy's research underscored the enormity of education problems in the United States, and she was certain that effecting any sort of systemic change would require starting big. She believed that reforming education to eliminate inequities had to be a sweeping movement, not a gesture, and se envisioned Teach for America as an important part of that movement. Her goals were audacious, but Wendy firmly believed they were attainable.

Wendy's trajectory reminds us that the gall to think big is as much about a deep base of knowledge as it is about vision. In order to address a problem fully, you need to learn every aspect of it, including ist history, trends, key statistics, supporting data, current and proposed policy measures, the economics of the problems, and the major players in the field. Once you have gained comprehensive knowledge of a problem, you can develop a vision that is grounded on practical strategies.

Wendy's approach to learning was an academic one: she used her college career to study educational inequities in the U.S. Through writing her senior thesis and shoring up the knowledge she had already gained from classes, her conference, and discussions with classmates, she was able to envision a solution to a problem close to her heart. But Wendy's approach is not the only one possible. Practical and experiential learning can be just as useful.

Wendy moved to turn her senior thesis into a funding proposal. She tracked down the addresses of some thirty CEOs and business leaders and requested meetings to ask for support. Wenday had never met any of the people she was approaching. She was not a recognized education expert. She had not yet graduated from college. All she had was a remarkable entrepreneurial spirit, coupled with a willingsness to do whatever was necessary to make her idea become a reality.

While her classmate celebrated their imminent graduation, Wendy put on a business suit and, proposal in hand, started taking the early train into New York City from Princeton to ask for money. Her thesis adviser asked if she understood how difficult it was to raise $25,000, let alone the $2.5 million Wendy had proposed as an initial budget. But by the end of the summer after graduation, Wendy had been given office space from Morgan Stanley in Manhattan, established a founding board, and received corporate support from the Mobil Corporation and a seed grant from Echoing Green.

Wendy aggressively set about recruiting, selecting, training, and placing in schools the 500 teachers who would make up the first corps of Teach For America. This large-scale beginning gave Teach For America momentum and a sense of national importance that Wendy believed was critical to attracting the most sought-after graduates. "Teach For America quickly attracted hundreds of people, who were drawn both to the core belief and idea of the importance of educational equity as well as the power and simplicity of the Teach For America mission," Wendy says.

A social movement – a collective action in which individuals, groups, and organizations unite to carry out social change – is often sparked when a large number of people realize that others share their values and desire for a particular change. One of the many challenges facing an emerging social movement is exactly how to spread the news that it exists. Teach For America created a visible outlet, enabling disparate groups that cared about the same thing to come together. Even though the business leaders who supported Wendy doubted that Teach For America could attract enough young applicants, they understood the crisis in our nation's public schools and felt compelled to act. The young people whom Wendy contacted had no expertise in the field of education, but as Wendy knew, they were looking for something meaningful to do with their lives.

Charismatic leadership, such as Wendy's rallies, forces and provides a voice calling for change. Although the leadership of one person is an important part of movement building, it is only one component. Social movements are grounded in time and place and are catalyzed when the right forces come together – forces beyond any one individual's control. Wendy says, "If I hadn't thought of this idea, I have no doubt that someone else would have."

Today, Teach For America fields over 4,000 teachers annually, who work in over 1,000 schools in twenty-two regions, with a goal to reach an 8,000 member corps by 2010. It took ten years to build a stable organization with 1,000 corps members per year, and another six to reach the 4,000 mark. Movement building and social change are long-term propositions. Wendy is in it for the long haul and continues to do the math.

Today, more than 12,000 Teach For America alumni work across the country, filling leadership positions in the fields of education, business, and policy. This small army of education reform activists fights locally, regionally, and nationally for educational equity. Furthermore, Teach For America has entered the consciousness of the younger generation. In 2006, Teach For America received almost 19,000 applications for its teaching program, including applications from 10 percent of the graduating classes of schools such as Spelman, Yale, and Dartmouth.

As Wendy marks her second decade at the helm of Teach For America, she is no longer a college wunderkind, and her organization is no longer a daring upstart. Teach for America is a mature, nationally recognized nonprofit organization with a $55 million annual budget and over 350 staff members. It is one of only twenty-one direct-service, nonprofit organizations (excluding hospitals, museums, universities, etc.) founded since 1971 to have a budget over $20 million. Wendy is projecting an annual budget for Teach For America of $100 million in the next five years. She is a seasoned nonprofit professional who has received much praise and many awards in recognition of her accomplishments, including the Citizen Activist Award from the Gleitsman Foundation, the John F. Kennedy New Frontier Award, Aetna's Voice of Conscious Award, and the Jefferson Award for Public Service. In addition to receiving six honorary doctorates, Wendy was the youngest person and the first woman to receive Princeton's Woodrow Wilson Award, the highest honor the school confers on its undergraduate alumni.

In the story of Teach For America's first decade, *One Day, All Children: The Unlikely Triumph of Teach For America and What I have Learned Along the Way*, Wendy provides a valuable "how-to" and "how-not-to" manual for aspiring nonprofit leaders. As the title of her book suggests, Wendy is anything but smug or self-satisfied, and she openly discusses the many mistakes that resulted in budgetary cash-flow problems, public-relations firestorms, and low staff and corps morale. One entire section of her book is appropriately called "The Dark Years." But is was through that bumpy process that she learned the importance of building solid organizational systems and instilling core values. Wendy's story reveals the power of the gall to think big. You press on because you must and because your idea for change truly matters.

* The Chapter is from a publication of Echoing Green:
Be Bold – Create a Career with Impact
By Cheryl L. Dorsey and Lara Galinsky

Young Volunteers as Social Entrepreneurs

Catherine Cecil, Youth Star Cambodia

Following three decades of conflict, Cambodia is rebuilding and changing quickly. After more than a decade of peace, Cambodia is still a young nation with many signs of positive improvement. The economy grew at double digit rates from 2004 to 2006[1] with significant growth continuing into 2008. The poverty rate declined to 35% in 2004 from 45-50% a decade earlier[2]. Cambodia faces serious challenges and significant opportunities. The time is ripe for the contributions of social entrepreneurs.

For example, Cambodia has a shortage of qualified experienced professionals, due in part to the fact that most professionals left Cambodia or died during the Pol Pot era. This shortage of skilled human resources is particularly acute in rural areas, where 91% of Cambodia's poor people live[3]. These communities need new ideas and fresh perspectives.

On the other hand, Cambodia has a growing youth population. A full 70% of Cambodians are under age 30. This population is also becoming more educated. More and more young people are graduating from universities each year. But at a time when Cambodia needs these young people and their passion and skills, the education system falls short of international standards, and employers say that that these young graduates lack experience. Many have few options for employment, leading to frustration and despair.

Youth Star Cambodia seeks to help fill these human resource gaps while developing the next generation of social entrepreneurs and leaders. The organization provides an opportunity for young people to gain skills and confidence while contributing to the development of Cambodia. Founded in 2005, Youth Star Cambodia recruits, trains and places young Cambodian university graduates to volunteer in underserved rural areas for one year. Ultimately, Youth Star Cambodia seeks to harness the energy and idealism of youth to solve Cambodia's pressing social problems. Youth Star Cambodia volunteers are role models for citizens in action and catalysts for community development.

Youth Star Cambodia's mission is to build a just and peaceful nation through citizen service, civic leadership, and social entrepreneurship. Our work is guided by the belief that building a just and peaceful nation is every citizen's right and responsibility, and that each individual can make a difference.

Youth Star Cambodia's vision statement focuses on three aspects of our work. Our citizen service vision is that soon all Cambodian youth will have the opportunity and want to serve their community and nation. Our civic leadership vision is that soon Cambodian youth will have the values, skills, and inspiration to be leaders for the common good. Our social entrepreneurship vision is that Cambodian youth will be catalysts for social transformation and bring creative solutions to the pressing social problems of Cambodia.

As budding social entrepreneurs, these volunteers face barriers within themselves and within their culture. Cambodia's hierarchical society discourages individuals from taking the initiative to contribute to society. "All relationships are hierarchically ordered. The hierarchy is expressed first in terms of age, then comes gender, wealth, knowledge, reputation of the family, political position, employment, character of individual and religious piety[4]." Another barrier is an aversion to taking risks. Cambodian proverbs say "do not reach for the stars" and "do not look over the mountain[5]." Cambodian society prizes conformity, in public and private spheres, "leaving little space for idealism, new thinking and new energy[6]." As a result, people often wait for others to act, instead of taking the initiative to become leaders themselves.

Cambodia's isolation from other countries during the 1970s and 1980s also continues to have a significant impact on the way Cambodians think and see the world. However, with globalization and Cambodia's growing participation in regional and international bodies, this is beginning to change[7].

Youth Star Cambodia seeks to help young volunteers overcome these barriers. First, the volunteers benefit from comprehensive training to help them build skills and confidence so they can meet the needs of communities. The training curriculum includes sessions with external experts who share best practices in development, ranging from concrete skills such as first aid to community development strategies. The volunteers also focus on their personal development through a range of exercises helping them to understand their own strengths and weaknesses. This training aims to help them contribute by working in four areas: supporting education and youth development, promoting sustainable livelihood, promoting health and well-being, and encouraging business entrepreneurship.

Volunteers also have training on citizenship. Youth Star Cambodia believes that active, engaged citizens are the key to Cambodia's future. But this concept is neither highly valued nor well understood. Although Cambodia's growing civil society organizations have succeeded in raising awareness about the rights of citizens, few focus on the responsibilities of citizens. Focus groups with young people show that they are unable to define citizenship. But all Youth Star Cambodia volunteers are motivated by their vision for the future of Cambodia, and they soon see ways for all citizens to contribute. Their volunteer service gives them an opportunity to develop their sense of citizenship.

Volunteer placements are driven by demand. Volunteers are placed with community partners, local groups such as farmers groups, business associations and schools, at the partners' request. These partners also make a commitment to support the volunteers by arranging their housing and meals, and by working with them hand in hand.

These relationships with local partnerships ensure that volunteers are integrated into community life. The volunteers spend the first month of their service meeting people in their new communities and mapping local strengths and challenges. The local partners play a big role during this period, as they take responsibility for ensuring that the volunteers make contact with people who will help them contribute to developing the community and build a sense of local ownership. Only then do the volunteers create an action plan, based on local needs, together with their local partners.

This combination of strong local connections and local input builds social capital, as highlighted in a recent study of volunteerism in Cambodia. "Volunteer involvement can have multiple social benefits, such as building social capital, civic participation and engagement. However, these effects will depend greatly on the extent to which the volunteers have freedom of action, and how they are conceived of as social actors, able to engage in and change their societies[8]."

Volunteers take on a range of projects, from building libraries to introducing innovative farming methods. They help local business associations establish bookkeeping methods and conduct major campaigns to promote safe migration in areas where vulnerable migrants have been cheated and trafficked. Common to their activities is their commitment to engaging others. Through their work with youth clubs, young farmers' groups, commune councils and other entities, the volunteers energize communities and provide hope and inspiration.

Even in its early stages, Youth Star Cambodia has gained insight into several key elements that help volunteers succeed as social entrepreneurs. One necessary quality is a highly developed sense of citizenship. This helps the volunteers find new opportunities to make a difference to their communities on an ongoing basis. Another ingredient of success is a creative and innovative approach. Volunteers with new ideas are warmly welcomed in these underserved communities. Finally, strong local connections are critical to the volunteers' success. These ties help volunteers tailor their solutions to their communities and gain the support they need to make meaningful social change.

Citizens in Action

On a personal level, volunteers develop a deeper insight into citizenship throughout the course of their service. When volunteer San Vannath first heard about Youth Star Cambodia "the word citizenship in Youth Star Cambodia's mission statement impressed me very much. But I did not clearly understand this word, and I wondered about each of our roles and obligations to our society and our country."

But when he began his service in Kampong Cham Province he discovered his own ability to become an active citizen. "I saw many problems and I knew it was my responsibility to help change things," he said.

And Vannath did indeed help change many things in his community. He tutored 53 students in Math and Khmer to help them catch up with their classmates. As a result, the percentage of students who were falling behind the class in grade 6 dropped from 20% to 11%, and the absentee rate fell by 30%.

But his biggest successes were in mobilizing others. He organized an environmental campaign by leading students to pick rubbish at the school yard twice a day. Soon other villagers followed their example. Small shop owners began to clean up the areas near their shops and to provide trash cans. The school began to provide trash cans in each classroom. And other community members began to clean up the areas near their houses. In all, Vannath mobilized 50 students and local leaders, including the village chief, school director and teachers.

Vannath set up a youth club to focus on life skills and healthy habits, as well as discussions on values. Among other activities, Vannath led a discussion on the consequences of early marriage, which often causes young people to drop out of school, and makes it more difficult for families to climb out of poverty. "The young people told me that their parents asked them to quit school and get married even though the young people did not have a clear plan. Our discussions gave them confidence to talk with their parents. Five young women succeeded in negotiating with their parents to postpone marriage so they could continue to study in secondary school and high school. Others were already engaged, so they made a clear plan for their future before they got married," he said. Vannath also organized a forum for students to discuss healthy relationships and the need for sensitivity towards others.

Now that he has finished his volunteer service, Vannath is still guided by his commitment to citizenship in his current job as a social worker with a local NGO in Battambang Province. "Volunteering allowed me to fulfill my obligation as a citizen, and I will continue to volunteer in the future. Now I like to tell people 'I am a citizen of Cambodia... and you'?"

Creativity and Innovation

Youth Star Cambodia volunteers use their passion and creativity to mobilize others to become active citizens. Many volunteers have engaged their communities in environmental cleanup campaigns by organizing events using rubbish in a creative way. Artists Leang Seckon and Fleur Smith, from The Rubbish Project trained the volunteers on organizing a Mode Somrahm (rubbish fashion show). Then the Youth Star Cambodia volunteers organized their own events.

At one fashion show in Prey Veng Province, 13-year-old Mean Srei Nuon proudly showed off her dress made of plastic, metal and leaves. After weeks of hard work with her youth club cleaning up the village and sorting through rubbish, she was a little nervous. A fellow youth club member was busy repairing the broken strap made from recycled drinking straws. Soon her fellow youth club member joined her onstage, wearing a necktie made from recycled drinking straws. Surrounded by posters made from recycled rubbish with messages about volunteers promoting development, the fashion show sent a powerful message to villagers of all ages who attended the event – and made everyone smile.

Other volunteers organized their own variations on this theme. In Kratie Province children flew kites they had made from recycled rubbish. Other celebrations featured displays of sculpture and pictures made from recycled rubbish.

Youth clubs devoted many weeks to picking up rubbish, cleaning the rubbish and brainstorming about ways to use these unique supplies.

As a result, young people gained a new appreciation of their ongoing responsibility to keep their environment clean. "Now they look at rubbish in a different way," said volunteer Oeur Phoumint.

These events were prominently featured at the 16 International Volunteer Day celebrations organized by Youth Star Cambodia volunteers on December 5, 2008. With festive tents, professional sound systems and well-rehearsed teenage MCs, the celebrations reflected and built on excitement about volunteering. Like other local celebrations, these events featured traditional dance performances, displays of produce grown by youth clubs, and displays of handicrafts made with local products in life skills courses. Youth clubs in many villages performed original drama presentations on social issues such as safe migration, domestic violence, the consequences of early marriage, and protecting the environment. Many celebrations had 100 or more guests of all ages, including local authorities, agriculture and fishery officials, monks, teachers, students and parents. In one commune in Kratie Province, students from five primary schools came to the ceremony.

As local volunteers received Good Citizenship Awards, the celebrations gave the volunteers an opportunity to reflect on their contributions. Srey Nich, age 17, from Prey Veng Province, said one impact of her volunteer work through the local youth club is that children and youth have better behavior, with "no more violence." Her neighbor Ros Ream pointed out that Youth Star Cambodia volunteers have helped farmers increase their rice production and helped families adopt healthy habits. "Now our kids are healthier," she said.

Volunteers reported a positive impact on their own lives as well. "I feel energized and honored that I can do something for my community," said Seng Ravin, age 16, from Prey Veng Province, who tutors younger children.

"I feel so good about my community," said Srey Rath, age 13, a member of the youth club in Orang Ov Commune in Kampong Cham. "Now I am encouraged by so many people because they all value me and my work. They say that even though I am still young, I have an ability to help people, especially children who need help to continue their studies to a higher level. Parents send their children to study with me because they see me as a role model."

Strong Local Ties

Youth Star Cambodia learned early on that volunteers are more successful when they have the opportunity gain the trust of their communities. This enables them to craft effective responses to community needs. Volunteer Phoeurk Saorathana followed two previous rounds of volunteers in her commune in Kratie Province. She was able to build on the successes of earlier volunteers, and to mobilize even more people to join her in her projects.

The first Youth Star Cambodia volunteers came to this community in 2005 had to prove themselves and demonstrate how volunteers could make a difference. Many people asked "what can volunteers do?" Others were even more skeptical. But as volunteers Surn Meng and Pech Choeurn met their neighbors one by one, they worked with their community partner to make an action plan tailored to the community – and became a part of the community themselves. The volunteers demonstrated again and again that they were working for the community interest and people began to trust them.

The volunteers discovered that it was very difficult for people in this area to earn a living. Many people drank too much alcohol and this often led to domestic violence. Villagers faced high costs for food because they relied on products transported from other areas. Education was not valued, and many girls did not go to school because the schools were far away. Young people got married at early age without full awareness of their responsibilities.

With guidance from their community partner Kong Sam Ath, also the chief of primary schools in Svay Chreah Commune, Meng and Choeurn knew that strengthening education would provide a path for addressing these challenges. They went to work in three primary schools. In community meetings, they told parents that educating their children would reap benefits for their whole families. "Before the volunteers came, it was really difficult for parents to see the advantages of sending their children to school, said Sam Ath. "If the local people tell them, they ignore us. But when people outside the community tell them, they listen."

Soon the volunteers saw results. A total of 1,800 children over age six registered for school, compared to 1,600 children the year before.

Choeurn and Meng were alert to new opportunities to encourage people – especially young people – to improve their lives. The volunteers pointed out the difficulties of early marriage at village and commune meetings. They asked commune authorities to refuse permission for marriage of persons under age 18, and the authorities agreed to their request. The volunteers also conducted a multi-pronged campaign to encourage people to drink clean water and formed a children's group to focus on life skills and literacy. Named the Green Club, this group shared information on planting vegetables and raising livestock.

Several months later, in 2006, Chap Veasna began his volunteer service in the same commune, but he worked in different schools. Like the other volunteers, he built relationships and mapped his community's strengths and weaknesses. Veasna realized that improving literacy would empower others to make further improvements. He worked with a local school director to prepare a school library and arranged a reading schedule for each class.

Veasna made a connection with his new neighbors when he shared his personal experience. "I am from a very poor family," he told them. "My mother raised pigs to sell at the market and it was very difficult. But she encouraged me to study and to complete a university degree." The number of visitors to the library rose as more children began to love reading.

Working through the library and the school system, Veasna took steps to reduce the school dropout rate. Veasna took his responsibility to each child seriously. One 14-year-old student, Sophea, told her teacher that she was quitting school because she needed to earn money to feed her poor family and her five siblings. Sophea faced another barrier as well – the distance to her school. She was finishing primary school, and the nearest secondary school was 10 kilometers away. But Sophea was a good student, so Veasna and Sophea's teacher talked with Sophea's mother about the value of Sophea's education and Veasna gave her his bicycle when he finished his volunteer service.

Sam Ath said this intervention affected more than one student. "If she stopped studying, it would a very bad model and every child would follow her," he said. "I feel proud because now I see a lot of parents send their daughters to study at the secondary school that is seven to 10 kilometers from home. Sophea has done a good deed by providing a positive example for other girls."

Following in the footsteps of the original Green Club, Veasna introduced local children to Sao Phat, a model farmer, so they could learn how to plant vegetables and sell them in the market. Sao Phat was pleased to help out, Veasna reports, and the children planted a garden at their school.

In late 2006, Saorathana and another volunteer arrived. By this time local people had a positive view of volunteers and a clearer view of what they could accomplish. With a strong base of trust and a good reputation for mobilizing people, these later volunteers were able to expand the scope of their work by mobilizing larger numbers of people and organizing bigger projects.

Once again, Youth Star Cambodia volunteers helped make up for gaps in the local education system. Saorathana taught English and other subjects when no other teachers were available. She traveled from five to seven kilometers each day, from village to village. But Saorathana's impact was dramatically increased when she inspired three teenagers to volunteer to tutor their classmates and weaker students. As one volunteer explained, "If Saorathana can travel a long way to teach, why can't I?"

Saorathana also challenged the members of her youth club to be creative. She started a campaign to build respect for local Traing trees, which are used in many ways, as medicine, roofing materials and lumber for making products such as chopsticks and fishtraps. "These trees have many special benefits, 'she said, "but I could see that people did not value these trees or take care of them."

With help from children at all five area primary schools and a secondary school, Saorathana and the local youth club conducted research on local proverbs about preserving trees and constructed exhibits on the trees using unusual art supplies from these trees. The showed their exhibit at a local event held to showcase life skills activities.

"We worked hard. And we were pleased to see that our project opened people's eyes," Saorathana said. "But the best part of the project was seeing how these young people came alive when they had a chance to be creative."

Saorathana and the children used unusual art supplies for the exhibit, such as woven mats and ropes for leading cows made from these trees. Sometimes the children were surprised. "The children asked me, 'Why did you do it that way'," Saorathana said. 'But they also said 'it's totally beautiful.' I told them 'that's what creativity is.' Their faces lit up when we made our flowers out of Traing leaves, and used fish strainers made out of Traing wood in our exhibits. As parents and other villagers admired our work, I asked the students how they felt. "We could never imagine that we could be so creative," they said and told me this was a fantastic project.

The youth club also produced a book about the Traing trees. Along with unlocking the creativity of the youth club and increasing respect for natural resources, the book won high marks from area schools as an educational tool. Sam Ath shared a copy of the book with government education officials, and other copies are available in local school libraries.

Local parents reported other benefits of this project as well. They told Saorathana that their children were more willing to volunteer their ideas to help the community. This experience inspired Saorathana as well. "When I think of these children and how their world expanded through their own creativity, I know that anything is possible," she said.

Both Saorathana and her fellow volunteer shared critical information with local people about health threats such as HIV/AIDS, bird flu and malaria. Based on the community's trust in her, Saorathana was able to raise awareness about more sensitive areas of women's health. She discovered that few pregnant women had prenatal checkups at the local health center because they were too shy. Saorathana advised them, "please choose a healthy life over your shyness." She also talked to young girls about female health issues.

Sam Ath sees lasting effects from all of these volunteers. Along with primary school attendance, secondary school attendance is up, from 150 to 188 students, with more female students than male students. Similarly, the number of area students attending high school students in a nearby town has increased from one to 12. Similarly, the rate of early marriages is down. Sam Ath has his own measurement system for early marriage: wedding invitations. Before the Youth Star Cambodia volunteers came, he would often receive 20 wedding invitations from secondary students each year, but now he only receives two or three invitations each year.

Local teachers have responded to the volunteers' hard work and positive attitudes as well. "Teachers start their classes on time and uphold higher standards of professionalism," Sam Ath said. "In the past our teachers would not even come to school on days when it was raining."

Some effects of Youth Star Cambodia volunteers are quite visible. Sam Ath notes that a year after Veasna completed his service, "our school garden is thriving, with water convolvulus, peas, eggplant, and lemongrass." Others have followed this example with vegetable gardens of their own. Several families are growing so many watermelons that they have arranged for a truck to take them to distant villages for sale.

Sam Ath also reports greater community engagement. More people understand and value their roles as citizens, he says, and participate in commune planning sessions, community cleanups and tree planting activities. More women are involved in these in community and livelihood activities as well, he said.

After three successive waves of volunteers, villagers have replaced skepticism with engagement.

Nuth observed that a lot of people are asking for more volunteers, but it is clear that they themselves have become volunteers, and demonstrated what citizens-in- action can accomplish.

Now in its fifth year of operation, Youth Star Cambodia looks forward to building on the work of these volunteers. The organization seeks more insight into the impact of social entrepreneurs in these communities, and on ways to improve it. It is clear that beyond Youth Star Cambodia's volunteers, Cambodian villages are filled with energetic and dynamic people who want to make a difference to their communities. Now Youth Star Cambodia's task is to inspire them and engage them in strengthening and further developing their communities.

Notes

1. World Bank (2007) *Sharing Growth: Equity and Development in Cambodia, Equity and Development Report 2007*, Bangkok, page 1.
2. Ibid., page 3.
3. World Bank, (2006) *Halving Poverty by 2015? Poverty Assessment 2006*, Phnom Penh, page 35.
4. Mysliwiec, Eva (2005) *Youth, Volunteering and Social Capital in Cambodia*, Phnom Penh, page 11, quoting   Ovensen, J., Trankell, I. & Ojendal, K. (1996) *When Every Household Is An Island*, Uppsala Research Report, Uppsala University, Sweden.
5. Mysliwiec, page 18.
6. Ibid.
7. Ibid.
8. Brown, Eleanor (2008) *Volunteerism: Harnessing the Potential to Develop Cambodia*, Phnom Penh, page 31.

Social Enterprise and Social Entrepreneurship: Tools to Achieve a More Balanced World

Kirsten Gagnaire, Social Enterprise Group (SEG)

Introduction

What would a world in balance look like? Is it possible to provide adequate food, water, and shelter for everyone without depleting our natural resources? Can we make the extraordinary shift in the way we live so that our planet has the chance to heal and become whole again?

We need a new approach, new tools to help us rebalance our world. We need to design an economy that is based on social and environmental benefits as well as financial ones. We need to harness the intellectual and technological advances we have made in the past 100 years and reassess their abilities to solve our problems rather than to add to them. We need social sector organizations that are financially viable, businesses that do good and entrepreneurs that do good business so that we can achieve balance for ourselves and for our planet.

Before technology and commerce significantly changed the way we live and our effect on both human and natural environments, Native Americans imagined, and lived in a world that was more in balance. The following story, reprinted from the *Bear Tribe's Self-Reliance Book* (Simon & Schuster 1998), tells the Fable of the Water Clan, a tribe that used innovative ideas to improve the world.

The Fable of the Water Clan

Once upon a time long ago some people traveled across the great Water in canoes that had giant sails upon them. These strange canoes were able to haul the many people coming in search of new land because the rulers in their old lands had become evil and selfish, and had taught the people to hate those who had a different language, or a different way of worshipping the Great Spirit. The rulers encouraged wars that made them profit but caused suffering and death to the people.

When they came to the land of our ancestors our people welcomed them and sat down with them in council and treated them as brothers and sisters. They passed the pipe, smoked, shared good thoughts and words together, and our people and the strangers gave gifts to each other. There was much happiness on the land.

The people who came across the water said they had need of new homes. Our people said "Come live with us and share our land and our ways and you shall be called people of the Water Clan." The people from across the Great Water looked at the ways of our people and saw that there was peace and plenty and that each man could worship the Great Spirit according to his own vision. So they accepted, with warm gratitude, the offer of our people. They learned to respect our system of government where chiefs and counselors sat together and made good decisions for the people.

The Water Clan told horrible tales of other lands, where men ruled for money and became corrupt. They said "This shall not happen here. Our chiefs, like yours, shall counsel for love of the people and they shall work together in the hunt or the fields with their brothers and sisters."

They told other stories of how people were put in prison because they stole when they were hungry, or killed or committed injury against their fellow humans when there were sicknesses in their minds. And they said "This is bad. It is better if we do as you do and feed the hungry and send people who are sick in these ways to spend time with counselors and medicine chiefs who can help them become well."

As the country grew, we founded warm-up centers together where people who felt upset or had problems could go and rest and be warmed up with love from the wise counselors who helped them to expand and find their balance.

As people moved westward they met more tribes of people who had other visions, and they said, "This is the vision for this part of the land. We must respect it. There are different chiefs here and they are loved by their people, so we will accept their knowledge and counsel."

The chiefs there told their people to take of the buffalo only what they needed for food and the people saw that this was good wisdom that would always leave buffalo for the children yet to come. A chief named

Sitting Bull said he had a bad dream that white men in blue coats came with fire sticks to kill and murder his people. The Water Clan people assured him this would not be, since this was a sickness they had happily left behind when they reached the shores of this new land.

As the Water Clan, along with members of some other clans, moved across the land they continued to meet new people until finally the people knew of each other from sea to sea. In some places people had large villages, but always they raised their food together about the village so that they remembered their balance with the Earth Mother. Each area had a council of chiefs who measured the value of any new ideas according to how they would benefit the people, the Earth Mother and the Great Spirit.

When a man called Ford discovered an invention that could move people and cultivate land, they said, "This is good if we use it well. We can raise food to feed hungry people in other lands, and we can move necessary items more quickly within our own land. This will enable the people of one area to visit with people from other areas so that we may learn from each other and our hearts may beat more as one." The Water Clan people thought of many inventions that became useful for the good of the people and which worked in harmony with the land, and the other clans said, "It is good that our new brothers and sisters came from across the water to join with us."

When the Water Clan members heard that the people in their old lands had gone crazy and made many weapons that killed many people they asked if they might bring these people to the counselors. This was done, and they were placed in warm-up centers until they learned balance. Then they were sent back to their own lands, and they taught this balance to others while they worked to rebuild the things their madness had destroyed.

Everyone learned a balance with the Earth Mother, and she became green and bountiful in her joy. The Great Spirit looked to the Earth where all creatures knew their place and purpose and was glad to see their happiness. It is good.

This is how it could have been. This is how it still might be for those people who learn to walk in love and balance on the Earth Mother.

Tools for Balance

The Water Clan paints a simple and beautiful picture of how the earth can be and the ways in which we have strayed from balance. Like social enterprise and social entrepreneurship, the Water Clan's fable envisions a world that weaves together innovation with benefit to society and the earth.

Social enterprise and social entrepreneurship are powerful tools that can help us achieve an economy where the value of new ideas and business is measured by how they affect our human and natural environments.

A **social enterprise** pursues a social or environmental mission using market-driven approaches to increase impact and sustainability. Social enterprises can exist in all sectors, business, nonprofit, government and philanthropy. As a field of practice, social enterprise is gaining momentum. Organizations such as Social Enterprise Alliance and the Social Enterprise World Forum, which serve the social enterprise field, are increasing in size and scope.

In the nonprofit sector, a typical example is an organization that starts a revenue generating business with the primary purpose of providing job skills and services to the clients they serve, e.g. people in recovery or who are transitioning out of homelessness. For these types of social enterprises, making a profit is typically not the main goal, although they often can generate enough revenue to help underwrite the cost of providing services, thus requiring less grant funding. Their mission is to operate a business that can provide important services to a population in need while generating some additional revenue to ensure their services can be provided over the long term.

In the United States, social enterprise can be found in some areas of government as well. Many municipalities run their park and recreational areas as social enterprises, generating revenue from user fees, concessions and corporate sponsorships or partnerships. Some government agencies require their divisions to create business plans and operate as profit generating businesses. For example, The United States Forest Service has an Enterprise Unit that focuses on "moving away from large staff organizations toward a model in which units that use their budgets to care for the land and serve people can purchase services they need from internal enterprises," (*The US Forest Service Enterprise Program: Reinvigorating Government* by Toni L. Stafford, 2007).

In the private sector, the creation, or restructuring, of businesses that are both socially and environmentally responsible is increasing. The U.S. Organic Trade Association's manufacturer survey notes that "The U.S. organic industry grew 21% to reach $17.7 billion in consumer sales in 2006." A new segment of the economy has emerged in the US and globally. In the US, it is referred to as Lifestyles of Health and Sustainability (LOHAS) which accounts for approximately 41 million

US adults who spend and estimated-$209 billion U.S. marketplace for goods and services focused on health, the environment, social justice, personal development and sustainable living.

Often it is the financial bottom line that causes a significant change in how business is conducted. For instance, the meteoric rise in fuel prices is causing many companies to restructure the way they produce and ship their goods; the old hippy axiom "buy local" makes good business sense and companies are seeking ways to produce goods closer to their end market. Add the benefits of lowering emissions and suddenly a company looking to increase their profits can jump on the "greenwagon."

However, consumers are increasingly demanding that their products come from companies that have true positive social and environmental impact, through fair sourcing, low carbon emissions, healthy working conditions, and similar factors. As consumers become more savvy about adverse business practices, they are becoming aware of attempts to green-wash certain products and services. The US Government's business.gov website states that "the most successful green businesses don't just sell the green lifestyle. They live it. Selling green means being green and this helps build your brand and image as socially responsible."

Going back to the Water Clan Fable, we can see that people are finally waking up to the creation of a world where inventions are "useful for the good of the people and which work in harmony with the land."

Social entrepreneurship is another vital tool to achieving a more balanced world. It is primarily focused on the social sector and focuses on applying entrepreneurial skills and thinking to solving social and environmental issues, rather than on selling products and services. The Skoll Foundation describes a social entrepreneur as "society's change agent: pioneer of innovations that benefit humanity." They describe a social entrepreneur as "distinct from a business entrepreneur who sees value in the creation of new markets, the social entrepreneur aims for value in the form of transformational change that will benefit disadvantaged communities and ultimately society at large.-Social entrepreneurs pioneer innovative and systemic approaches for meeting the needs of the marginalized, the disadvantaged and the disenfranchised – populations that lack the financial means or political clout to achieve lasting benefit on their own." As in the fable of the Water Clan, the value of a social entrepreneur's idea is based on how it benefits the people and the earth.

Fortunately, there are hundreds of social entrepreneurs who are pioneering entrepreneurial approaches to help achieve a more balanced world. The 2006 Nobel Peace Prize winner, Muhammad Yunus, developed the Grameen Bank which provides credit to the extreme poorest and helps lift people out of poverty by helping them develop their own micro enterprises. Jim Fruchterman, a 2008 MacArthur Fellow, founded Benetech which applies technology to benefit society, such as providing reading machines to the visually impaired. Bill Drayton founded Asoka, an organization that pioneered the field of social entrepreneurship. Ashoka currently supports over 2000 social entrepreneurship fellows in 60 countries around the world by helping them scaling their innovative solutions to many of our most pressing challenges (water, education, housing, health care, etc.)

Tools in Action

There are many empowering case studies from the field of social enterprise that prove that a shift in how we do business can bring greater balance to our lives. Located on the sunny, warm island of Oahu, HI, MA'O Organics is a social enterprise that was developed to maximize impact by focusing on the triple bottom line of social, environmental and financial benefits. In comparison, The Bainbridge Graduate Institute, located on a cloudy, cool island off the coast of Seattle, WA was started by a small group of social entrepreneurs who saw a problem in society and set out to scale a solution for addressing it. Both organizations, while serving widely different communities, illustrate how it is possible to successfully embody the Water Clan way of life.

MA'O Organics is a social enterprise that helps youth reconnect to their community and to the land while learning necessary life skills. Nestled in a picturesque valley in the largely native community of Wai'anae on the west side of the island of Oahu in Hawaii, the mission of MA'O is to grow organic food and young leaders that will lead to a sustainable Hawaii.

Considerable political, social, cultural and economic barriers exist on Oahu that have led to overdevelopment and the resulting depletion of natural resources. Additionally, there is a serious disconnection of the native youth from their families and the community. Native Island youth have the highest rates of teen pregnancy, school suspensions, incidents of substance abuse, and juvenile arrests than their non-native counterparts while native Hawaiians have the highest rates of preventable disease including diabetes, heart disease and some cancers. Once a self-sustaining agriculturally sophisticated culture, there is now little access to fresh, local fruits and vegetables on the island; almost 90% of the organic produce found in the markets is imported.

MA'O Organic Farm, through its nonprofit parent, the Wai'nae Community Redevelopment Corporation, strives to develop a comprehensive and living local food system – educating youth, fighting hunger, improving health and nutrition, growing the local organic agriculture industry – to empower their community and help its residents move towards greater self-sufficiency. At the core of MA'O's cultural, educational, and economic development strategy is a concerted effort to assist Wai'anae's youth in becoming more self-sufficient and entrepreneurial. This approach prepares local youth for leadership roles critical to development of productive and sustainable food systems for the people of the Wai'anae Coast. They do this by using a multi-faceted approach:

1. **Operating a revenue generating organic farm.** MA'O is a self-sustaining organic farm of almost 11 acres. It is operated by Kikui & Gary Maunakea-Forth, a small staff, the local youth who participate in their programs, and community volunteers. Kikui & Gary are model social entrepreneurs who combine sound environmental practices with broad community impact while remaining financially viable. They strive to have the farm be a model of self-sufficiency and entrepreneurship for the youth they serve.
2. **Selling local produce via retail and wholesale venues.** MA'O makes its produce available to their community by being a regular vendor at the local farmer's market. They have become a reliable and affordable way for the community to access healthy, local foods that are an integral part of improving the health of Hawaiian natives. Most of Hawaii's organic produce is shipped from the mainland, sending money out of the local economy and bringing in produce that has a shorter shelf life and is considerably more expensive. MA'O is helping to reverse this trend by also selling to local supermarkets, including Hawaii's first Whole Foods Market; and their produce can be found on the menus of many of Honolulu's upscale restaurants.
3. **Providing opportunities for youth engagement and leadership.** MA'O has many ways to engage youth. Middle school students participate in culturally-based, hands-on workshops that are delivered through in-school workshops. Students from the local high school run a half-acre organic garden in cooperation with MA'O. All students have the opportunity to learn about organic gardening, how to eat healthfully and about entrepreneurial approaches for selling the produce. Additionally, MA'O has an intensive food systems and organic farming internship program for high school students. Finally, the Youth Leadership Training college internship programs provides students with the chance to obtain an Associate of Arts degree from Leeward Community College while engaging in a hands-on organic farm management program at MA'O.

MA'O Organics provides a powerful example of how a social enterprise can be used to positively impact a community, contribute to the health of the planet and generate revenue for long-term sustainability.

The Bainbridge Graduate Institute (BGI) was founded in 2002 by a group of social entrepreneurs: Elizabeth & Gifford Pinchot III, Jill Bamburg and Sherman Sevrin. BGI's mission is to "infuse environmentally and socially responsible business innovation into general business practice by transforming business education."

BGI's founders felt strongly that traditional Masters in Business Administration (MBA) programs were not adequately preparing future business leaders for the catalytic role they could play in the development of a socially just and environmentally sound world economy. By offering one of the first MBAs in Sustainability, BGI has helped inspire a major shift in the traditional academic approach to business education. In addition to their MBA program, BGI provides assistance to other academic institutions who were seeking to integrate sustainability into their core programs.

By 2004, the first class of 18 students graduated from BGI. In just four years, the school has grown to over 200 students and now offers certificate programs in Sustainable Business and Entrepreneurship & Intrapreneurship in addition to the MBA in Sustainability. The college attracts faculty and speakers from all over the world, including sustainable business pioneers such as human rights activist Van Jones, author Amory Lovins (Natural Capitalism), progressive investor Leslie Christian (Upstream 21) and Seventh Generation CEO Jeffrey Holander. BGI is currently adding a monthly Activist-in-Residence to its Leaders-in-Residence and is expanding the Sustainable Industry Concentration program to include five industries:

- Agriculture & Food Systems
- Community Economic Development
- Energy Solutions
- Green Building
- Outdoor Industry

BGI subscribes to a community-based model where student involvement plays an integral role in the development of the culture, curriculum and growth of the college, enabling the students to learn by doing. Graduates have gone on to work for global corporations such as Hewlett-Packard and Recreational Equipment, Inc. (REI), while others have started their own sustainable businesses, working to create more systemic solutions to environment, education, health and community issues.

BGI is revolutionizing the way business leaders learn, think about, and apply their knowledge to help create a more socially just, environmentally sustainable and profitable world. As their model grows, their impact will grow – through the work of their graduates and the graduates of other programs that have been inspired by BGI's success.

Summary

We can regain our balance, though it will take some work. Fortunately, as we have seen, there are powerful and effective tools for affecting significant change in the way we conduct business and address difficult social issues. Social enterprise provides us with a more holistic approach to applying the principles of the market economy to help us become more socially, environmentally and economically stable. While social entrepreneurship enables us to develop and scale solutions that utilize innovative technology and solutions that create sustainability, both culturally and ecologically.

Existing businesses need to reassess their impact and consider how to incorporate social enterprise practices into their services and products. Entrepreneurs starting new businesses should make the benefits of sound social and environmental decisions a key component of their business models. Individuals, communities, and organizations that are faced with difficult challenges can look to a social enterprise approach for help with solving the pressing issues of our time. Activists can em-brace entrepreneurial models and become the social entrepreneurs that scale the innovative solutions to help bring us back to balance. Individuals can make a difference for their communities; communities can make a difference for the world and we can all live in peace and plenty.

Part C

Valuable Tools for (Social) Entrepreneurs

Social Entrepreneurship:
The Balance of Business and Service

Pamela Hawley, UniversalGiving

Over the past decade, Social Entrepreneurship has been leading the charge as "the innovation" which will impact our communities. It's generating a new wave of leaders: Social entrepreneurs are seen as a catalyst to deliver high impact results in our communities. At its best, social entrepreneurship is a balance of business and service.

I'd like to share part of my journey in practicing social entrepreneurship while founding UniversalGiving™, as well as identify the **Top Three Factors of Good Social Entrepreneurs**, which may help new and existing social entrepreneurs.

At the age of 12, I had a moving family experience in Mexico: I'd been walking in the community with my father, and we stumbled upon a cult-de-sac of maimed, begging, unwashed children. I was shocked and deeply hurt to see humanity in this condition. I remember something to the effect of 'UNACCEPTABLE' being stamped across my mind. It's stayed with me every sense, this relentless drive to serve and help provide opportunities for others.

At that point I decided to devote myself to our communities and began volunteering. As time progressed, I enjoyed the service component, but was challenged by the lack of efficiency in some organizations. Critical in my development as a social entrepreneur was this balance between 1) service and compassion and 2) an organization led by business principles. It's important to note, however, that inefficiency can happen in nonprofits, forprofits, governments, churches. It's not fair to label nonprofits inefficient; it's not the legal structure. It's about positive, effective management and governance, which can take place in any entity. It's about leadership, which led me to Bill Drayton and Ashoka.

I'd heard of Bill Drayton and his early work on social entrepreneurship in the 1960s, which I had found very inspiring. At such an early stage, he seeded and mobilized thousands of social entrepreneurs all over the world. The emphasis was on evaluating the qualities of leadership of the self-starter entrepreneurs, who due to their leadership, ethics and integrity, led and managed effective initiatives that could be scaled worldwide. I also studied and met with Jed Emerson at the Roberts Economic Development Fund, which focused on nonprofits running a business, or businesses providing a social good, which provided some very successful social models.

A pivotal moment surfaced in graduate school: An extremely inspiration speaker and serial social entrepreneur, Peter Samuelson, challenged us to consider 'entrepreneurial philanthropy' as a new way to operate. At the time, he stated, "It's either social entrepreneurship, or entrepreneurial philanthropy" – the ability to create and scale high performance organizations and services in a rapid fashion. We must adopt this mindset that we can effect change across the world with increased acceleration and efficiency. I'll accept nothing less. Do it today."

I was hooked, inspired; mouth gaping. I had finally found my calling: the marriage between my drive of soundly run business, and still serving the community! As I spoke with my father and shared my inspired, teary revelation at age 25, he encouraged, "That's great! Now how do you get paid for this?" Good question. To get it right, I knew I wanted to be a part of creating the social entrepreneurship leadership and culture. At that point I completed my graduate studies in communications, bent on being a social entrepreneur.

In the meantime my volunteering graduated to the international front, striving to understand and serve people who were living on 16 cents, 50 cents or $1 per day. I volunteered in many countries, including rural communities four hours outside of Bangalore in India, helping with microfinance; working on sustainable farms in Guatemala; in the earthquake crisis of El Salvador. From these experiences, I wanted to find a way that people could find *quality, trusted ways to give and volunteer.* I founded UniversalGiving™ a web-based organization which helps people give and volunteer with the top-performing projects across the world.

People simply choose a country of interest (such as China or Thailand) and an area of interest (such as education or the environment) and find a list of vetted opportunities to which they can donate money or give their time. We don't take a cut on the donation and 100% of your dollar goes to the project. We help thousands of people find the most trusted and effective way to give and volunteer in more than 70 countries across the world.

In order to establish trust, we developed an in-house proprietary Quality Model™ which vets all projects and organizations with a ten-stage vetting process. As I volunteered, I saw that trust was paramount. I was continually asking myself: How can we highlight the excellent work of these local leaders? How can we provide assurance and trust to our donors, so that they know they are giving to effective projects? As with any endeavor, there were organizations and leaders that were stellar, and others that were faltering. We had to find the best of the best, and our Quality Model™ reflects numerous objective and subjective factors. Our goal is to increase the top ways of giving and volunteering all over the world.

Part of our quality process, which we see as integral to our standards as social entrepreneurs, revolved around the culture from which we operate, Silicon Valley. We developed our Quality Model™ partially based on venture capitalists: How would they review a new idea? First, they would review the business plan. If they liked the idea, the very next thing they would ask is: "Who's leading it? Whose the management team?" And so we ask ourselves the same questions. To this day our NGO partners and leaders are featured on UniversalGiving™ in part due to their leadership qualities and the long-term personal relationships we have with them.

Critical to our social entrepreneurship model, UniversalGiving™ has two services: A public service that allows anyone to give and volunteer, and a corporate service that generates revenue. Since our public service is free, we needed to determine what was of value about our service, and how we could provide that value to paying customers. UniversalGiving Corporate (UGC) is a customized service helping companies manage their global Corporate Social Responsibility (CSR) Programs. UGC helps ensure that a company's giving and volunteer programs are successful all over the world. We help with strategy, operations and management, and NGO vetting. Our goal here is to help the company establish strong relationships in their local community, which also increases corporate brand image; employee attraction/retention; and client attraction/retention. We focus both on improving a company's bottom line while also serving the community.

For example, in our work with Cisco Systems, we help launch their Civic Councils, which are employee-led community engagement teams. UniversalGiving Corporate helps their employees increase giving and volunteering in each local city that employees live and work. We help determine strategy and operations; we help with virtual management of more than 30 Civic Councils across the world. We operate on their behalf, fielding questions from employees and helping ensure NGOs are vetted and uploaded into our web application. We scale the positive work and best practices from each Civic Council city to the next one, compiling a best practices manual for future Civic Council management. In essence, we are helping Cisco be top leaders in CSR because we establishing long-term relationships and management plans that solidify their presence in the community. Critically important, Cisco values this work and pays us accordingly, which in turn is invested back into UniversalGiving™ to help serve more of our impoverished communities. In that way we offer two services: One that is free to the general public; one that is paid for by our corporate clients. The end result is a solid blend of service and business that embodies social entrepreneurship.

The Evolution of Social Entrepreneurship is Timely

The landscape today necessitates that Social Entrepreneurship evolve even more rapidly, with an eye on results. We now have increasing pressure for forprofits, nonprofits, and hybrids to incorporate both business operations and a commitment to caring about our community. The goal is to provide demonstrable results, but at the same time to not lose the heart and soul of serving. Add to that an increasingly challenged global economy, the recent loss of $1 trillion in value people's assets, and decreased funding sources, and the import of social entrepreneurship delivering results increases.

The definition of social entrepreneuship varies; each story is unique. However, the following **Five Key Questions To Ask Regarding Social Entrepreneurship**, as well as **Top Three Factors of Good Social Entrepreneurs**, can provide some helpful guidelines regarding your initiative.

Five Key Questions to Ask Regarding Social Entrepreneurship

1. Is the organizational structure nonprofit or forprofit?
2. Does the organization generate revenue?
3. Does the organization plan to achieve full profitability or sustainability?
4. What is more important: The actual service provided or the revenue?
5. Are its services scaleable across the globe?

These are questions that should be asked and debated, thought through and discussed, particular to each new or existing social entrepreneurship initiative. In a quick summary, I'd posit that social entrepreneurship can be forprofit or nonprofit, but, the entity should generate revenue. The service should be valued by both the heart – and the head. The ideal goal of a social entrepreneur would be to achieve positive cash flow, generating revenue to cover all and more of its expenses, along with delivering worldwide impact for its intended communities.

For UniversalGiving™ we chose nonprofit, because I felt it would best build the UniversalGiving™ brand and our integrity as a social entrepreneurship organization. Since we are dealing with philanthropy and volunteerism, we wanted to solidify our pure intent of serving our communities. We wanted no questions as to our motives. Secondly, if we did need to make a decision between the service or the revenue, we could choose service. I could choose to help an impoverished person over revenue. If we were forprofit, I'd say one's responsibility must be to the revenue first, due to your organizational structure and responsibility to shareholders.

We do and should generate revenue from corporate clients. We plow it right back into our public service, making it stronger and more personalized so that donors, volunteers and NGOs who visit the UniversalGiving™ website can benefit. Therefore, it is indeed a delicate balance. Every social entrepreneur needs to find the unique model which fits their social entrepreneurship motive best.

Top Three Factors of Good Social Entrepreneurs

In summary, I'll leave you with the top three factors of being a good social entrepreneur:

1. **Value Both Service and Business.** You have to love the service you are providing (such as serving impoverished people across the globe), as much as running a business. You need to engage with and be inspired by leadership, strategy, sound business planning, revenue. The days of the nonprofit leader who has only heart… are over. Heart is wonderful and needed, and must be balanced with a strong desire to execute with business principles.
2. **Generate Revenue.** Simply leading a well-run nonprofit, in my opinion, is not enough to be called a social entrepreneur. Truly think through the value your service provides. How can it be monetized? In UniversalGiving's case, we provide the initial service for free to the public. Anyone can give and volunteer, with 100% of their donation going to the project or nonprofit of their choice. But we then approach companies, provide them value with our international CSR management and NGO expertise, and get compensated for doing so.
3. **Scale Your Efforts.** If you aren't thinking about how your venture can replicate itself in other areas, then I'd state it's not social entrepreneurship.

The highest definition of social entrepreneurship designs its products and services to grow in multiple populations, in hundreds of cities across the world. Local organizations and nonprofits are always needed and should be encouraged. But to reach an advanced level of social entrepreneurship necessitates looking beyond your locale.

Social Entrepreneurship is an exciting and now practical concept. Let's accelerate the rate at which we can achieve good in our communities, through both sincerity and heart, as well as sound business principles and planning.

At UniversalGiving™, that translates into our vision: "Create a World Where Giving and Volunteering Are A Natural Part of Everyday Life."™ We want everyone to think about giving and volunteering, just as they would pay their cellphone or heating bill. It should be natural. And so is social entrepreneurship – as one part of the solution to providing increased service, effectiveness and impact in our world.

Giving Donors What They Need

Andreas Rickert, Bertelsmann Stiftung

THE BERTELSMANN STIFTUNG was founded in 1977. In keeping with the longstanding commitment of its founder, Reinhard Mohn, the Bertelsmann Stiftung is dedicated to promoting the public good as an operating foundation.

It focuses on the fields of education, economic and social affairs, health, and international relations. Furthermore the Foundation promotes the concept of philanthropy and wants to bring fresh momentum to civic engagement.

Efforts to Solve Immense Social Challenges are Coming from State, Market and Civil Society

Despite many positive developments in recent years, societies all over the world are faced with immense challenges: Overpopulation and hunger, social distress and a lack of education and the immense ecological problems with which the entire world is currently dealing, disease, drought and struggle for economic resources, care for the disabled, the elderly, children and all of those who cannot help themselves. Even though with very different intensities, there is hardly a country that is not facing these challenges.

Sometimes it seems that the fight against these challenges is a battle that cannot be won. And it is tempting to accept that this is simply part of humanity. However, the fact that this fight is being fought nevertheless is also a part of humanity. And the hope for a better life is the most deeply rooted human trait of all – and an important and worthwhile battle.

When looking at all these big words, it is of crucial importance to talk about who the participants in this battle are. Who is making an effort to improve the living conditions in the entire world?

Efforts are coming form all three sectors: (1) The state and international organizations, (2) the market and business community, and (3) the civil society and philanthropic world. Even though all three segments will be looked at separately in the following, it is very important to point out, that the best results are often achieved, when the boundaries between these three sectors are tiered down, when state, market and civil society work together to fight social problems.

Nations – some well-positioned, others less – are attempting to improve the lives of their people. The welfare state in Europe, the strong focus on free market laws in the Anglo-Saxon countries and all the various approaches in the countries and societies with less income are trying to support individuals in their fight for a more humane life. Nations are coming together in order to be able to better achieve this objective in times of increased globalization.

Companies are helping their fellow man. Admittedly they do not always do this and sometimes they even act against the interests of common welfare. But let us make no mistake: Innovation and discovery, efficiency increase and goal orientation do not always only serve shareholders and their bank accounts. Mohammed Yunus is a shining example when it comes to combining common welfare and economic activity for improving the lives of people. But we do not have to just focus on this popular example. In fact, there are hundreds, thousands of other companies who run their business in a very responsible way. They help in solving social challenges either through their products and services directly or by investing a significant amount of their revenues in CSR-activities. And these CSR-activities go way beyond the being a marketing-instrument.

Talking about CSR-activities, the link to the civil society, to philanthropic engagement is made. Worldwide you can observe that charitable commitment is increasingly regarded as a solution for many national and international social challenges. Often the state and the business community are unable to adequately master the countless challenges for people's wellbeing. This need not necessarily points to a failure on the part of the state or the business community or to a fundamental failure of structures and regulations. Both of these entities – the state and the business community – simply cannot take on all of the challenges and combat all the problems. So the activities of the civil society should not be regarded as makeshift, but as a complement.

And it is a great pleasure and satisfaction to see that there is a multitude of remarkable examples of this force within civil society: in educative and health programs, in environmental protection, in reducing poverty or in the arts and culture - philanthropic commitment helps to ensure that many services can be provided, either at all or extensively.

In the following, two questions regarding the charity sector will be further discussed:

- Who are these philanthropically engaged individuals?
- What do they need to even better fulfill their highly important activities?

Social Entrepreneurs and Demanding Donors – New Types of Social Actors are Changing the Civil Society

All these success stories we know from the civil society depend on the tremendous engagement of individuals. They are engaged – either through financial contribution or time commitment.

Individuals driven by philanthropic interests have always been there and have helped to fight the problems of their age. However, in recent times we can observe that there are new types of philanthropic players:

We find social entrepreneurs.* They are using methods and management styles known from the business world in order to achieve their social goals. They are looking for professionalization, they are interested in best-practice transfer, they are scaling up their approaches in order to address their social aims in the most effective and efficient way. Along with social entrepreneurship, a new type of donors is emerging. One aspect is the amount of money available to donations. And here we are not only talking about Bill Gates and Warren Buffett or similar affluent people all over the world. Wealth has penetrated into the middle classes of many of our societies. Millions of people all over the world have substantial means and are without material worries. These people are rich when we compare them to the majority of people in the world, and they are willing to share their money. In Germany alone, private individuals donate between 2 and 3 billion euros per year and foundations provide some 7 billion euros for charitable causes. Using international benchmarks, we can predict that even more money would be available for social activities if donors find stimulating and motivating structures meeting their needs.

Together with New Philanthropy Capital (NPC), Wise Partnership and Scorpio Partnership, the Bertelsmann Stiftung conducted a survey on this subject. We surveyed benefactors and major donors in order to better understand what is important when they consider giving money to charitable causes.

In general, the motivation to give is highly cause or project driven, with 90% of the sample giving because of their experience of a particular issue or for historic reasons. The desire to "give back" to the community, the capacity and wish to see change, and the disillusionment with government all motivate donors to give. Donors want to support something specific. They do not want to just do something general for the environment, for education or for arts. No, they find it important to assist a specific project, or an organization with their money, concrete entities, people, those in need. They like to see the faces of those they are helping, and to see concrete results.

In order to keep their momentum and to transfer the motivation to action, donors seek advice and information before, during and after the donation. And this kind of help and orientation is often not provided by lawyers and bankers. Therefore, the donors as well as their financial advisors often discover donating as a process which represents something new to them. Besides guidance on the process of giving, donors are looking for oversight, control and trust concerning the money being donated. They would like to have choices in order to identify a project which perfectly fits their philanthropic interests. And they strive for certainty, that these projects use their money in a responsible, efficient and effective way. Ultimately, they want their money to make a difference; they want to make an impact. Their support should help people to be better off than without their help. They are keen on seeing this and they want to have someone who will tell them objectively that their support is making a difference. They ask for a kind of "reporting" we know from the business world.

Most of the interviewees in the survey find the philanthropic experience rewarding and stimulating. Individuals typically increase their level of philanthropic involvement with time. But crucially, this growth in commitment comes on the back of positive experiences. In many cases philanthropy is a reinforcing cycle of involvement, positive experience, renewed commitment, deeper understanding and further success.

All these described characteristics of donors may be due to the fact that many of these donors have been very successful in their professional business lives. Thus, they are applying the same principles when it comes to private donations. For them it is important to see their money being used in an effective and efficient manner. They are interested in making information-based decisions regarding their donations in order to achieve impact with their donations.

And there should be someone to fulfill these wishes of those who donate. For the wellbeing of those who deserve to receive assistance.

The key learning points can be summarized using the following quotes:

- "The more money I give, the more I must rely on those who are familiar with this area and who can advise me."
- "The more money I give, the greater my interest in knowing that it is being put to effective and efficient use."
- "The more money I see put to good use, the more I will give."

Over the course of the study we heard one sentiment repeatedly:

- "It should not be so difficult to give money."

Lack of Transparency Hinders the Full Power of the Civil Society

It should not be too difficult to give money. However, there is limited transparency in the charity sector guiding the donors and channeling the funds to the good social activities. On a broad scale, the social entrepreneurs and the social investors are usually not coming together based on objective information in order to make the best of their philanthropic engagement.

On the one side, the non-profit organizations want to present themselves to potential donors in order to raise more funds and they want to improve their activities via professionalization and exchange. On the other side, the donors want options regarding the content and region of quality assured non-profit organizations.

In spite of these requirements regarding supply and demand, in many countries there are only a few instruments today that support donors in their decisions regarding charitable investments. Often, orientation for donors is just provided with respect to governance structures and financial aspects of major charities or via the self-commitment declarations of various umbrella organizations. And rarely, orientation guided by the social impact of charitable organizations is provided by independent, third parties.

In view of this, both the social investors as well as the organizations competing for funds complain of the high costs of transactions that result from the process of teaming up with each other.

Information-Based Matching of Donors and Social Entrepreneurs Promotes New Impulses to the Civil Society

In order to meet these widespread structural deficits, means are needed to provide orientation for those who want to financially support good social projects and organizations.

Consequently, reliable tools providing transparency about the performance and quality of social engagement are desirable. However, the evaluation of social activities is not a trivial task.

Certainly, we can count how many malaria immunizations have been performed, how many hours have been spent with the disabled, how much money has been received by literacy campaigns. But who will tell us if things could have been done differently, done better? In business, the competition tells us when a company has not employed the resources in a target-oriented manner. The competitor's goods and services will simply be better and less expensive in this case. This is hardly feasible in the philanthropic realm; at least a way to do this has not been evident up to now, or, if you wish, there are very few "marketable" tools to independently and objectively measure how well philanthropic organizations perform their work.

Because of this, the Bertelsmann Stiftung has developed an analysis method for the non-profit sector. This method is based on a tool used by NPC in London and has been further refined and adjusted to the German market by bringing together experts from academia and representatives of many of the major stakeholders of the non-profit sector in Germany.

This analysis of non-profit organizations is build on a tested and transparent method, is characterized by appreciation for these organizations, is based on the voluntary nature of these organizations, is feasible for these organizations, is carried out with experts in methodology and the respective field. The evaluation itself comprises nine categories, analyzing on the one hand the effectiveness of the organization itself and on the other hand the effect of their activities on target groups and society.

Specifically, the analysis categories are:

1. Vision, strategy and planning
2. Decision-making processes and personnel management
3. Finances and controlling
4. Fundraising
5. Governance and committees
6. Objectives and target groups
7. Concept and approach
8. Monitoring and evaluation
9. External effect regarding success in reaching target groups and society at large

The assessment process comprises three steps:

1. A detailed questionnaire
2. Review of documents
3. On-site visits

The results of the analyses are presented to potential donors via portraits on positively evaluated social organizations considering all of the nine categories mentioned above. In addition, to provide comprehensive overviews on specific areas of social engagement (e.g. musical education for children), reports are composed providing detailed background information on the respective social field (e.g. relevance for society, theories of change, alternative approaches to addressing the problem) along with portraits on various organizations that are engaged in this field. Such an assessment tool provides donors with the independent and objective advice they need to better understand the work of good charitable organizations and how they achieve impact. These portraits and reports make it easier to give away money.

But not only the donors benefit from these analyses. The process has been tested with dozens of not-profit organizations by now, and the feedback from them is surprisingly positive. Most of the organizations welcome this transparency, and use the analysis to learn about their own strengths and weaknesses, to eventually improve their way of working. After all, many social entrepreneurs who work for charitable organizations are always asking themselves. How can we work even more effectively? An objective perspective from a third party will give these people many answers to their questions. In addition, an overview of other organizations with similar interests is also important to charitable organizations. How do others do it? What can we learn from them? These questions are answered all too rarely. And the evaluation approach provides the option to link social organizations so that they can learn from each other.

So far, the described initiative of the Bertelsmann Stiftung has only reached a limited number of charitable organizations and donors. However, it could be scaled up with partners from state, market and civil society creating a new dynamic in the non-profit and not-for-profit sector, which could ultimately lead to a qualitative and quantitative growth of the civil society.

Fortunately, similar approaches providing orientation for donors and social investors can be observed worldwide. All these initiatives should not be limited by national boarders; they should be linked in order to support best-practice transfer among social entrepreneurs and to allow information-based money flow to charitable causes all over the world – to fulfill the donors' wishes for a wide range of options for their engagement and to reach all good charitable projects, wherever they take on the fight against social challenges.

However, even if such a network of intermediaries all over the world would promote a more transparent, more efficient and effective charity sector, one thing is clear: we will not defeat hunger or disease. At least, this would seem an utopian ideal in this day and age. Nevertheless, together with the efforts from the state and business, all philanthropists – social entrepreneurs, volunteers, donors, benefactors, social investors – help in the best way they can to advance the condition of mankind and make people's lives a little more positive, a bit happier, slightly less worrisome.

Strategic Marketing for Social Entrepreneurs – How to Make Tough Product and Service Decisions

Jerr Boschee, The Institute for Social Entrepreneurs

Introduction

Maintaining an appropriate balance between social impact and financial viability is the sine qua non of social entrepreneurship. Dr. David Rendall calls social entrepreneurs "tightrope walkers" because they are constantly hovering in mid-air between their social purpose and marketplace realities.

The definition of "appropriate" varies from organization to organization, but the existence of a double bottom line that emphasizes both social and financial returns forces social entrepreneurs to continually make difficult decisions about which products and services to offer and which markets to pursue.

The process is never more important than when a social enterprise is developing its strategic marketing plan – and it can be agonizing because it demands that Board members and senior managers practice triage.

The First Rule of Entrepreneurship

Management-guru Peter Drucker famously advocated killing products and services if they were not number one or number two in the market. Rather than trying to be all things to all people, he wrote, you should concentrate on doing the best job possible in a few, carefully chosen areas. If you do not, he warned, you will be unable to give customers the attention they deserve because you will no longer have the necessary time or resources.

Drucker's advice runs against the grain of the traditional nonprofit mentality, but most nonprofit managers eventually do admit they are trying to serve too many masters. And, as they morph into social entrepreneurs, they realize that the first rule of entrepreneurship is contraction.

Of course, triage requires a social enterprise to be honest with itself – exceedingly difficult for any organization, nonprofit or otherwise. But the results have been worth it, and the ultimate winners have been clients and customers. Social entrepreneurs have discovered that reducing their number of products, services and target markets has actually enabled them to serve more people and to serve them better, because they've had the time and resources to expand their most effective and needed lines of business and to carefully introduce new products and services.

Making strategic marketing decisions, however, is more difficult for a social entrepreneur than it is for either a traditional nonprofit or a commercial business, both of which are primarily concerned with a single bottom line. A traditional nonprofit will continue offering products and services that have a significant social impact even if they lose money; most commercial enterprises will not. Social entrepreneurs, on the other hand, are equally concerned with both bottom lines, and that means they must simultaneously analyze the social impact and financial viability of each product and service – and only then make decisions about which ones to expand, nurture, harvest or kill.

"The Strategic Marketing Matrix"®

"The Strategic Marketing Matrix for Social Entrepreneurs"® consists of two levels. Level One is a quick-and-dirty way for Board members and senior managers to think about the intersection of social impact and financial returns.

"The Strategic Marketing Matrix for Social Entrepreneurs"®: Level One

	Positive financial returns	Negative financial returns
Significant social impact	EXPAND	NURTURE
Minimal social impact	HARVEST	KILL

Level Two is an expansion of Level One that requires more rigorous analysis. It measures the relationship between the degrees of social need being addressed and the anticipated financial results:

"The Strategic Marketing Matrix for Social Entrepreneurs"®:   Level Two

	Significant potential profits	Modest potential profits	Modest potential losses	Significant potential losses
Critical social need	EXPAND	EXPAND	NURTURE	*KILL
Sizeable social need	EXPAND	EXPAND	NURTURE	*KILL
Minimal social need	HARVEST	NURTURE	KILL	KILL
Zero social need	KILL	KILL	KILL	KILL

How can a nonprofit discover where a specific product or service falls within the matrix? The first step is market segmentation, the subject of the next section. Then the nonprofit must answer the following three fundamental questions about each market segment, questions we will explore in greater depth on subsequent pages:

"Will it make a difference?"

- What is the level of social need? How many people in the market segment actually need the product or service, regardless of their ability to pay? And how critical is their need?

"Can we win?"

- What are the critical success factors associated with designing, developing and delivering the product or service for this particular segment?
- What environmental forces will play a role? Will they be positive or negative? How helpful or damaging will they be? Do we have the capability to capitalize on the opportunities and mitigate the threats?
- Who are the primary competitors? How do we rank against them in terms of critical success factors and environmental forces? Can we be number one or number two in the market?

"Are the numbers right?"

- What is the potential size of the market segment in terms of dollars? And what is the opportunity within the segment – is it growing, remaining flat or declining? How much has been exploited? How much of the competition's share is vulnerable?
- What are the fixed and variable costs? Will we make a profit or lose money? How much? When?

Market Segmentation

Many nonprofits resist the need to practice triage. The process is taxing, and emotions run high. But even social entrepreneurs who understand its importance and summon the courage often start from a false premise. During my coaching sessions with nonprofits around the world, I frequently ask Board members and senior managers what they believe is a simple question: "How many programs do you offer?"

Few have ever gotten the answer right. Here's the list provided by a Texas nonprofit helping people with developmental disabilities live independently:

- Home care services
- Adult day care centers
- Independent living skills
- Social skills training
- Education programs
- Residential programs
- Transportation services
- Respite care

In other words, eight programs. Or so they thought. Actually, they had 31.

Why were they so far off the mark?

Because every program has both a "subject" and a series of "predicates" — a product or service and a collection of target markets. It is not enough to say a nonprofit offers home care services for "people who are developmentally disabled." To effectively allocate resources, the nonprofit must divide that mass market into more useful segments. Doing so is called market segmentation, and the criteria for dividing a consumer market (business to business markets have criteria of their own) include such things as:

- **Demographics** (e.g., age, income, gender, marital status, family size, occupation, education, income, nationality)
- **Geography** (e.g., nations, states, regions, counties, cities, neighborhoods, climates)
- **Psychographics** (e.g., customer lifestyles, activities, interests, social class, personality characteristics, comfort with technology, political leanings)
- **Customer behavior** (e.g., frequency of purchase, sensitivity toward price, levels of desired quality, and so on)

Once the people in Texas decided "age" was their best segmentation strategy, it became evident they were operating many more programs than they thought, because each of the 31 market segments in the chart on the next page requires a different marketing plan, operations plan, break-even analysis, employee skill levels, and so on.

	Infants	Pre-teens	Teens	Adults	Elderly
Home care services	X	X	X	X	X
Adult day care centers			X	X	
Independent living skills		X	X	X	X
Social skills training		X	X	X	X
Education programs	X	X	X	X	X
Residential programs			X	X	X
Transportation services			X	X	X
Respite care services	X	X	X	X	X

Triage, then, required them to move from the macro level (eight programs) to the micro (31) before making any decisions about resource allocation. And, as we saw previously, "The Strategic Marketing Matrix for Social Entrepreneurs"® contains four possible allocation strategies:

- Programs high on both the social impact and financial viability scales should be **expanded** and deserve the bulk of an organization's resources
- Those that are high in social impact but haven't yet achieved financial viability need to be **nurtured**
- Those that deliver positive financial returns but have minimal social impact should be **harvested** to generate resources for the programs being expanded or nurtured
- And, of course, those low on both the social impact and financial viability scales should be **killed**

As a rule of thumb, programs to be expanded should collectively receive about 50 to 70 per cent of a nonprofit's resources. "Nurture" programs should receive about 20 to 40 per cent, and "harvest" programs whatever remains. Ultimately, once they completed the research we will be describing in the next few pages, my clients in Texas made the following decisions, killing 14 of their 31 market segments:

	Infants	Pre-teens	Teens	Adults	Elderly
Home care services	EXPAND	EXPAND	HARVEST	EXPAND	EXPAND
Adult day care centers				EXPAND	EXPAND
Independent living skills		KILL	NURTURE	NURTURE	KILL
Social skills training		KILL	KILL	KILL	KILL
Education programs	NURTURE	NURTURE	KILL	KILL	KILL
Residential programs			KILL	EXPAND	KILL
Transportation services			KILL	EXPAND	KILL
Respite care services	HARVEST	NURTURE	HARVEST	KILL	KILL

"Will it Make a Difference?"

Market segmentation is a relatively straightforward process, but determining the level of need in a particular segment is tougher than most social entrepreneurs expect. It's not just a numbers game.

For example, which is more critical to a local hospital:

- Infant car seats used to transport newborn children to their homes (2,000 families use the car seats each year)?
- Or incubators, ventilators and intravenous tubes for premature babies (200 families need them each year)?

Clearly, equipment for premature babies rises to a higher level of need than car seats for healthy newborns.

When I first began teaching strategic marketing in 1989 and insisted my clients measure the level of social need in each market segment, I asked them to choose from a five-point scale:

- Is there a critical need? (a score of "5")
- Is there a significant need? (a score of "4")
- Is there some need? (a score of "3")
- Is there minimal need? (a score of "2")
- Is there zero need? (a score of "1")

It didn't work. Almost all the people in the room insisted every market segment deserved a "5"!

And it's understandable. Decisions of this sort are fueled by the passions of the people involved, and most people in the nonprofit sector are reluctant to classify anything they do as less than critical. They loathe the idea of turning anybody away, so when they see somebody in pain, they try to help. Somebody else is hurting? Start another program. These folks need help? Start another program.

But classifying everything as equally critical makes it impossible to allocate resources responsibly — so I eventually began challenging my clients to practice triage: No more than 20 per cent of the social needs should be considered "critical," no more than 20 per cent "significant." Most who accepted the challenge discovered two things: It was one of the most emotionally wrenching experiences they'd ever had — but it was also one of the most liberating, because they'd given themselves permission to be candid, often for the first time.

Practicing triage successfully may mean bringing in neutral observers to provide a broader perspective. Some of the most helpful have been men and women who are themselves successful entrepreneurs. Even then, however, there are no hard and fast rules about which social needs should be considered critical or significant. Making the final decisions may require members of a senior management team to compromise with one another, but the overall goal is to achieve a consensus everybody can live with.

Determining the level of need can telescope the strategic planning process somewhat. Anything that receives a score of "1" can be immediately discarded – and the same may be true of those that receive a score of "2" unless there's a real chance to harvest.

"Can We Win?"

Once social entrepreneurs are convinced the level of need in a particular market segment is sufficient to proceed, the next step is to analyze competitive strengths and weaknesses. To do so, they need to answer the following three questions:

What are the critical success factors associated with delivering this product or service to this market segment?

- Obviously, every business must have a strong management team, a powerful positioning strategy and sufficient resources. But the "critical success factors" we're talking about here differ from one type of business to another. Possibilities include price, volume, convenience, speed, dependability, reputation, intermediaries — and any number of others. There are typically four or five that specifically apply to each type of business, and if you don't identify them correctly and compete effectively, your business will fail.

What environmental forces are having or will have a positive or negative impact on your ability to operate the business successfully?

- What we are seeking here are the large-scale, fundamental forces that pose threats and shape opportunities, and they are generally demographic, economic, technological, political, regulatory or sociological. Most of the time, you can't control them, but you'll need to be prepared to either capitalize on the opportunities or mitigate the threats. You'll need to identify the forces, decide if they're positive or negative, determine when they're likely to occur, estimate how sizable their impact will be — and, most importantly, decide what to do about them.

Who are your primary competitors and how do you rank against them in terms of the critical success factors and environmental forces?

- It's not necessary to identify all possible competitors, just the three or four that pose the greatest threats.

Here's what a typical competitive analysis matrix might look like (the number of critical success factors and environmental forces will differ from one type of business to another, and the weights and rankings will naturally vary depending on the type of business and the strengths and weaknesses of your competitors). See Matrix on the next page.

Here's how to develop a matrix of your own:

- Decide which critical success factors and environmental forces to measure
- Determine how much weight to give each of them — the total must equal 100 per cent
- For each factor and force, rank yourself and your four leading competitors one through five, with "five" representing the business in the strongest position (if you only have three leading competitors, use a one to four scale)
- Do the math — multiply the percentage for that line item by the scores you've assigned to yourself and to each competitor
- Add up the columns — the results will give you a rough idea of how you rank against your toughest competition (in this case, you are the best positioned to succeed, but only slightly ahead of competitor "D")

"The Competitive Analysis Matrix
For Social Entrepreneurs"®

	Weight assigned	Competitor A			Competitor B			Competitor C			Competitor D			Your business		
		RANK	SCORE		RANK	SCORE		RANK	SCORE		RANK	SCORE		RANK	SCORE	
CSF#1	20%	5	1.00		2	.40		1	.20		4	.80		3	.60	
CSF#1	10%	3	.30		2	.20		5	.50		1	.10		4	.40	
CSF#1	10%	1	.10		3	.30		5	.50		4	.40		2	.20	
CSF#1	15%	3	.45		1	.15		2	.30		5	.75		4	.60	
EF#1	15%	5	.75		2	.30		3	.45		1	.15		4	.60	
EF#1	15%	1	.15		2	.30		3	.45		5	.75		4	.60	
EF#1	15%	1	.15		5	.75		2	.30		3	.45		4	.60	
TOTALS	100%		2.90			2.40			2.70			3.40			3.60	

To compute a score, multiply the rank times the percentage for that line item

The key word in that last bullet, of course, is "rough" — this is simply a first cut to help you assess your competitive strengths and weaknesses. The next stage would be a more detailed analysis to confirm or invalidate your rankings, and that might take a few weeks or months. Once your review is finished, however, you'll have some tough decisions to make. If you're not number one or number two in a particular market segment, should you even take the planning process any further?

"Are the Numbers Right?"

The Plains Indians knew the truth of it: If you're riding a dead horse, your best bet is to dismount.

Unfortunately, in the nonprofit world, we resist the idea of abandoning a moribund product or service.

Instead . . .

- We lower standards (so dead horses can be included)
- We change riders
- We appoint a committee to study the dead horse
- We visit other nonprofits to see how they ride dead horses
- We provide more funding to boost the dead horse's performance

In the previous pages, we've been laying the groundwork to help social entrepreneurs make difficult strategic decisions about which products and services to expand, nurture, harvest or kill. In other words, to help them decide which horses still have life in them — and which ones don't.

In this section, we'll delve into the final question social entrepreneurs must answer before deciding whether to pursue a specific market segment. The level of need might be compelling, and we may have clear competitive advantages. But are the numbers right?

An informed decision will depend on two factors:

The size and direction of the market

- How many dollars are available to purchase the product or service? And how is the market trending – is it growing, remaining flat or declining?

Potential profit margins

- What are the fixed and variable costs? How long will it take to reach break-even?

Estimating the potential size and direction of a market segment requires careful research, and one way to do it appears below. The sample comes from work done a few years ago by one of my clients, a nonprofit that provided personal care services (e.g., cooking, cleaning, bathing) for elderly people confined to their homes.

**"The Market Size Calculator
For Social Entrepreneurs"®**

PAYMENT SOURCES	PAYMENT SOURCES	FINANCIAL ASSUMPTIONS, RESTRICTIONS	ANNUAL DOLLARS AVAILABLE
Medicaid	800	Maximum allowed: 10 hours per week at $10 per hour	$4,160,000
Personal insurance	400	Average annual maximum: $5,200 per person	$2,080,000
Adult children	300	Average per customer: 10 hours per week at $12 per hour	$1,872,000
Personal savings	300	Average annual amount: $2,000	$600,000
Corporate benefit	100	Average annual benefit: $5,200	$520,000
Other government sources	200	Maximum permitted: 10 hours per week at $10 per hour	$1,040,000
Miscellaneous	50	Average: $100 per week	$260,000
TOTAL	n/a	n/a	$10,532,000

Here's how you can create a calculator for each of *your* target markets:

- In column one, identify every possible type of payment source (the people running the personal care service had seven)
- In column two, calculate as accurately as possible the number of potential users in your catchment area (some customers will be able to draw on more than one payment source)
- In column three, describe the financial assumptions and restrictions associated with each payment source (the personal care people ran up against a number of government mandated limits – for example, at the time they did the analysis, Medicaid would pay for only ten hours of service per week per person at a maximum rate of $10 per hour)

- In column four, do the math – multiply the number of potential buyers by the financial realities (in the sample, there are 800 people eligible for Medicaid reimbursement at a maximum of $100 per week – or a one-year total of $4.16 million)

The total size of your current market will appear in the bottom right-hand corner of the grid. But remember: Only a fraction of the dollars are currently being spent. The rest are up for grabs – and even some of the dollars currently flowing to competitors could be re-directed your way through effective marketing and sales strategies.

Now create a second chart for the same market segment – but set this one three to five years in the future. By doing so, you can get a preliminary idea of whether the market will become increasingly attractive or stagnant.

If the amount of money available in a particular market segment is miniscule or heading in the wrong direction, it raises a testy question: Should we invest resources in that segment or direct them elsewhere?

However, there's one more step to be taken before reaching a final decision. Determining potential profit margins and break-even points are subjects beyond the scope of this essay (and best left to number crunchers). But there is an important point to be kept in mind: As we saw in the Level Two matrix near the beginning of this essay, many social entrepreneurs will decide to continue offering a product or service even if it does not seem to be worth it financially – because there will be compelling social reasons to do so. When they make that decision, of course, they will be depending on other sources of revenue to keep things propped up: Charitable contributions, government subsidies, or profits from another product or service.

Conclusion

Ultimately, every social enterprise has two fundamental challenges: To do the right things (strategic marketing) – and to do them right (operations). This essay has been focused on the first of those challenges, daunting as it may be to think about practicing triage. Strategic marketing is an attempt to shake up the organization – but not to shake it apart. In fact, strategic marketing may be the only thing that holds a nonprofit together in an increasingly competitive world.

Teekampagne –
"Citizen Entrepreneurship" for a
Meaningful Life

Guenter Faltin, Tea Campaign, Stiftung Entrepreneurship

Teekampagne: A Quick Overview

Teekampagne ("Tea Campaign"), founded in 1985, is not a well-known company because it spends so little on advertising. Nevertheless, it has become the largest mail order tea business in Germany. According to the Tea Board of India, it has been the world's largest single importer of Darjeeling leaf tea since 1998.

The idea for the company goes back to the "social entrepreneur" Gottlieb Duttweiler, founder of the "Migros" stores in Switzerland at the beginning of the 20th century. Duttweiler's goal was to provide pure, unadulterated products at an attractive price,through a business model that cut out layers of middlemen between producer andconsumer. For this blending of social vision and market economics, he was fiercelyattacked by both socialists and capitalists. One camp was defending its doctrine, the other its profits.

The name "Teekampagne" derives from the fact that originally, back in 1985, we sold our tea in "campaigns" – i.e. only at certain times of the year and only in certain places. Since tea keeps well for long periods, we encouraged our customers to buy their year's supply at one of these "campaign" events. Today, our Darjeeling tea is available year-round, or as long as supplies last. But then as now the term "campaign" speaks to our economic vision: to enable our customers to buy pure Darjeeling tea at an extravagantly small price. This vision requires that we "campaign" to educate consumers about our concept: we limit ourselves to one kind of tea, so that we can buy in large quantities and import directly from India, and we sell in large packages; specializing in Darjeeling tea allows us to carry out the strictest inspections and select the very best quality. Informed consumers are our most loyal partners. In fact, they "campaign" for us by word of mouth, saving us from using traditional marketing methods, thus lowering our expenses and the price of the product for themselves. Our customers are our collaborators; their understanding of the economic process has been a necessary condition for our success.

At the cost of small inconveniences (limited choices, planning ahead, putting in a year's supply), customers get an exquisite product at a low price. What, then, is the product?

It is named after the mountainous district of Darjeeling, on the slopes of the Himalayas in northern India. Darjeeling tea is considered the best tea in the world. It is cultivated at extreme altitudes, on steep slopes, under intensive sunshine in a generally cool climate. This gives it a distinct and unique flavor. The natural harvest quantities are limited.

Quality is paramount. Before we buy, we conduct many inspections to insure the best quality – a quality which requires the use of much and highly qualified labor to create and maintain. In addition, we look into our growers' use of agricultural chemicals, even in the case of organically grown leaves, to deter fraud. Each batch of tea is checked several times for hundreds of chemical residues (herbicides and pesticides), and we only buy the very cleanest teas. The results of our chemical tests are published on each package – we were the first tea company in the world to do this (even though many told us this would only frighten customers). The customer can also trace where the tea in each package comes from and when it was plucked. In addition, we have long campaigned for producers to do without chemical pesticides and fertilizers altogether; by the year 2010, all of our teas will be organically produced.

The practice of "sustainable development," of course, has many dimensions and cannot be limited to reducing the use of chemicals, reducing packaging, and reducing transportation. Importantly, in Darjeeling, a sufficient tree population is essential to halt soil erosion on its steep slopes. With this in mind, Teekampagne initiated and still finances a reforestation project entitled, "Save the Environment & Regenerate Vital Employment" (Project SERVE). In 1996, the World Wide Fund for Nature, India, agreed to manage our project locally, affirming our efforts with its international prestige.

Unfortunately, what is marketed as "Darjeeling" is not always Darjeeling. The Tea Board of India, the official Indian tea authority, has estimated that up to 40,000 tons of tea are sold world-wide under the name of "Darjeeling," although the district itself only exports 10,000 tons a year. To protect itself against this blending of Darjeeling with cheaper tea from other areas, the Tea Board introduced a special trademark, certifying that the tea sold with this trademark is 100% pure Darjeeling.

We were the first tea company in Germany to be awarded this seal of purity. We decided to use it as our company logo, instead of creating one of our own, to help with the planters' efforts to prevent adulteration of their Darjeeling with teas from low-lying areas. (All marketing experts considered this a foolish decision).

With this, we practice fair trade in a different and more comprehensive way than is usually conceived. In addition to using the trademark and protecting the purity of "Darjeeling," we finance a reforestation project, and we also pay higher prices than other traders would if they purchased 400 tons a year. And there is an additional, important aspect: we don't charge our customers higher prices for fair trade. Instead, our business model allows us to charge lower prices by breaking with expensive conventions (advertising, expensive packaging, etc.).

The education reformer Ivan Illich who I got to know in the early 1980s, used to argue vehemently against charging extra for fair trade. In this practice, he argued, the customer pays not only for the product but also contributes to an invisible "charity box," a modern version of buying "indulgences" (paying money to save your soul) – a trade that Martin Luther was already inveighing against. Although charity has some positive effects, it does NOT challenge the business models that put pressure on commodity prices in exporting countries and inflate prices for consumers at the other end. Since it does not represent a systemic change of business practices, it is also not sustainable: it may stop when the charitable giver's attention is drawn to another urgent need. We practice fair trade with a different method: we do not charge the consumer so that we can feel good about ourselves; instead, we challenge costly conventions, and the savings benefit everyone.

"Trade, Not Aid" is an effective and sustainable way of benefitting the region of Darjeeling as well as our customers and partners. We wanted to help create a trading situation, using market principles, that benefits both the producer and the consumer.

There is much research to demonstrate that in developing a regional economy which has the potential to survive, charitable donations and political subsidies often do more harm than good. Our aim is to raise consciousness about, and increase the demand for, genuine high-quality tea; embracing the Indian trademark as the sole guarantor of genuine Darjeeling quality is an effective strategy in support of Indian tea producers. A better quality will be achieved through hiring more labor, which increases some production costs, but will result in disproportionately higher sales revenues for the producer. Higher prices for better-grade tea, on the one hand, and greater demand for labor, on the other, allow the influential trade unions in Darjeeling to negotiate better wages and working conditions.

One tangible result we observe is that the employees on the Darjeeling plantations already enjoy better working conditions relative to other parts of India. High-quality production is also important for another reason: cheap mass production puts a downward pressure on prices worldwide, creating a glut in which supply exceeds demand. Neither the consumer nor the producer benefits from the creation of an inferior, adulterated product.

Such a product also tends to suffer from the "terms of trade" problem: as long as a finished product is created in the buyer country, exporters of raw materials will find it difficult to get a decent price. In the case of tea, merchants in the buying countries do this by blending teas of different qualities and places of origin, as well as by creating a variety of flavors through aromatic additives. By contrast, Teekampagne buys and markets Darjeeling as an end product. There is a much smaller span between the price paid to the producer and the price charged to the customer, while the overall cost to the consumer remains low. This is a "win-win" concept that benefits all sides. Our customers, too, can feel good about their cup of tea, knowing that their purchase sustains the people of Darjeeling.

Anyone Can: How I Got There

Although I was attracted to the field of economics quite early, starting at age 14 to invest my pocket money in the stock market, this was regarded as an inappropriate, even evil, activity in small-town Bavaria of the 1950s, and my family and teachers were emphatic in their disapproval. Naturally, I went on to study economics – only to find that the university curriculum had managed to turn an exciting subject into a boring and meaningless chore. I finished my coursework quickly, completed a doctoral dissertation in order to savor university life a little longer and, at age 31, as a sharp critic of how economics was taught, found myself being offered a tenured professorship, with a lifetime job guarantee from the government. When I accepted this position, I promised myself that I would study and teach the subject in a way that would keep my students awake and engaged. I already considered entrepreneurship, in its combination of theory and practice, the most vibrant field in which to bring economics to life, and I thought long and hard about starting a company. But how? I pored over the question which kind of business might offer good prospects. During visits to Tanzania and India, I was stunned to see how much more people have to pay for products like coffee, sugar, and tea in Germany, compared to the prices paid for them in the producing countries. In the case of tea, especially, the difference was huge. With only rudimentary knowledge about the tea business, I began to crunch numbers for tea and compare them with those for products in other fields. It turned out that the tea trade had very little price competition and relied on very traditional methods. After I analyzed the costs of trading tea, I realized that by challenging a number of conventions in the tea business, I could create a business idea that might (and did) look crazy to everybody else, but made superb economic sense: one variety of tea; only big packets: "buy your supply for a year." What looked like a joke at the beginning became a big success story. I learned that you can conquer a well-established market with a good idea; that the quality of an idea is more important than the availability of resources; that you do not need to know everything about business administration to succeed as an entrepreneur; that imagination and disciplined persistence trump everything else. I learned that (almost) anyone can be an entrepreneur. And I learned that you can not only keep your students awake, but that you can also have fun and do a lot of good at the same time.

Puzzling Out Simplicity

Neil Churchill, an entrepreneurship expert, once said that for a good idea to turn into a reality, up to 50,000 pieces of information need to be processed. It may take up to 10 years before an idea turns into a successful startup.

The history of ideas, experiences and insights that created Teekampagne resembles a puzzle, put together both playfully and persistently, and it certainly took years before the pieces came together in the simple, yet elegant picture we can see today. Some of the first pieces came about when I was a student at St. Gallen business school in Switzerland: I shopped at a Migros store, where one Swiss Franc bought you two and half chocolate bars. How come? In his early years, Duttweiler, selling from trucks, had rounded off prices to whole numbers (to save time on giving customers change), which resulted in charmingly odd product weights and measures. And why was Duttweiler so fanatical about purity of products and value for money? Why did he succeed, contrary to all conventions and expectations? My travels abroad added more pieces, leading to my discovery that the high price of tea in Germany was a function of expensive packaging and complex distribution systems. But how could one convince customers to choose only one kind of tea and buy enough for an entire year? Could one succeed in the marketplace by appealing to customers' reason, rather than distracting them with promises? Was it possible to educate, rather than seduce, the customer? To create (and rely on) economic literacy, rather than count on customers' ignorance? Treat the customer as a true business partner, rather than a prey?

Our initial gamble was that customers would reward an effort to enlighten them about their own best interests; that they would embrace a new concept which would offer them significant advantages. At its very core, this was an attempt to create the economic framework for a new, rational simplicity. Today, Teekampagne has over 180,000 customers, 93% of them by word of mouth.

One kind of tea; large packages; direct import and direct sale; purity; ecology; transparency. Seems simple. Why was this a radical idea? How can simplicity become a business concept?

Reasoned simplicity is indeed central to our business venture and to our philosophy of entrepreneurship. Think creatively, choose consciously, live wisely: these ideas can be found in Eastern philosophy, as well as among the ancient Greeks, in the tradition of the Enlightenment, but also among the 19th century Romantics. One of the thinkers we have found inspirational is Henry David Thoreau (1817-1862) of Concord, Massachusetts, best known for his book *Walden, or, Life in the Woods* (1854). Thoreau tells us that the richness of life consists of rich ideas and insights, not of an accumulation of material things. We should possess and consume few but excellent things. Teekampagne has embraced this idea. We offer "luxury through simplicity." In doing so, we not only make excellent tea available at a reasonable price. We also propose a new, and yet old, philosophy of life, which includes intelligent economics and consumption.

Rational simplicity is crucial to a person's well-being, as well as to our planet's survival. Declining resources, along with overpopulation and pollution, make a return to simpler approaches to life an absolute necessity. Proponents of simplicity enrich their lives by unburdening them. They try to calm "this chopping sea of civilized life" by choosing wisely among the thousand-and-one items offered daily. "'Simplicity, simplicity, simplicity'! I say, let your affairs be as two or three, and not a hundred or a thousand; instead of a million count half a dozen, and keep your accounts on your thumb nail," Thoreau advises. The message sounds astonishingly modern: live with a few excellent things, and live more deliberately.

Breaking With Convention: Simply Better Economics

"Simplicity" brings up some images that raise skeptical eyebrows: the well-situated professor advocating asceticism, or the holy man in his hair shirt; even the admirable Gandhi at his hand loom is not everyone's idea of the good life. To keep your eyebrows at rest, let me spell out how the principle of rational simplicity actually makes for better economics and for a superior enterprise. Here are some key features of our business model:

1. Simplicity means saving on unnecessary costs (e.g., packaging), while focusing on the most important functions (e.g., purity, transparency). Avoid waste! In our current project, the CO_2 Campaign (importation of high-efficiency, energy-saving light bulbs), the Chinese factory that makes the bulbs also packages them in the exact same cartons in which they arrive on the German customer's doorsteps. No additional repackaging (common in conventional distribution systems) occurs along the way.
2. Simplicity means efficiency: polishing away at the business model, until everything irrelevant (merely conventional) has been removed. The key aspects are in plain view.

3. Simplicity means plain speech, factual information, rather than advertising lingo. Customers are treated as rational beings; they are informed, not manipulated.
4. Simplicity means responsibility: satisfying a customer need with a good product, rather than creating a need that may be frivolous, wasteful, or even hurtful.
5. Simplicity means being clear about one's cause. If it is a social cause (e.g., environmental responsibility, fair prices, etc.), its cost should be borne not by the customer but through a rational business model that produces savings. These savings then support the cause.
6. Simplicity means helping the customer understand how things work: economicmechanisms as well as processes of production and distribution. An enlightened customer who can explain to others why Teekampagne can deliver great tea at low prices becomes an ally and ambassador for the company.
7. Simplicity means respecting the intelligence of others.
8. Simplicity means avoiding unnecessary complexity. Many founders fail because they are overwhelmed by the challenge of complexity that comes with growth along conventional business models.
9. Simplicity means taking the long view. This sounds like a paradox: of course we could increase our profits quickly by selling inferior teas, adding inexpensive flavoring (which German law would even allow us to call "naturally identical aromas"), and giving them fantasy names ("Tropical Dreams"). But in the end, we would become like all the others and lose our competitive advantage. We would also lose our identity and our integrity. Taking the long view requires the discipline to resist temptation.

Finally, rational simplicity acknowledges the fact that we live in a global economy that is characterized by fierce competition, by a never-ending battle for customer attention. You can seek that attention with gigantic marketing budgets – or you can gain it by being different, by being unconventional, by being clearly and unequivocally on the customer's side. Customers respond with respectful affection and become durably attached to your company; they become a community. This is the way of the future.

In the end, rational simplicity means better economics.

I am an economist. Some have called me an idealist – not intending to pay me a compliment. If what I have described is indeed "idealism," it is simply the belief that reason will have the upper hand. Our company's continuing success proves that this is not an unreasonable assumption.

Teekampagne and the Notion of "Social Entrepreneurship"

"Social Entrepreneurship" is a concept that seeks to de-scribe how social problems and social needs can be addressed with the tools and methods of business entrepreneurship, such as creativity; opportunity recognition; unbureaucratic procedures; looking beyond resource constraints; focus on the customer or client; 'can-do' ambition and resolute optimism. Although the concept arose out of an academic discourse about philanthropic and not-for-profit enterprises, it has now expanded to include a discourse about the non-individualistic ends served by for-profit enterprises and about the social responsibilities and/or obligations of business in general. I would even go so far as to speak of a "convergence theory": every enterprise should be conceived as a "social enterprise" in some sense; for-profit and not-for-profit enterprises should have more in common than is suggested by the fact that the one seeks to maximize profits (and distributes them to owners or shareholders), and the other seeks to optimize service to its cause.

I am troubled by the word "should," however. It smacks of the kind of moral admonition that spoils so much of the discourse about business ethics. People (and businesses) quickly tire of being told what they "should" do; it is much more effective and sustainable in the long run to acknowledge and appeal to their self-interest: to show them what they can do that benefits both themselves and others. In the case of social entrepreneurship, it is more instructive to look at businesses that already function well as social enterprises, and to figure out what they do.

Universities could be one example. In the United States, private universities are technically not-for-profits, but many have for-profit subsidiaries whose revenue stream helps to lower the cost of tuition and fees. Is Harvard University a business or a charity? It is both. With its need-blind admission practices, it will educate anyone with sufficient talent, regardless of that person's economic resources. Is it run like a business? Absolutely. Does this business serve a greater good? Indeed it does.

The search for conceptual commonalities between for-profit and not-for-profit enterprises recognizes that all good enterprises go for a cause, that they make meaning. The focus on commonalities may also help us around the intellectual trap of claiming altruism as the sole spring of not-for-profit economic activity; we can acknowledge the legitimacy of self-interest as a motivation for economic engagement, while pointing out that there is such a thing as enlightened self-interest that includes but transcends economic individualism; that seeks to serve the interests of multiple constituencies. "Cui bono? Who benefits?" may be a more pertinent question to ask about an enterprise than whether it distributes dividends or pays taxes.

In the for-profit business world, too, it is worth looking at businesses that function as "social enterprises." But what does that mean? Does it mean "giving back" some profit to a local community? Does it mean supporting a social cause, either from the company's profit, or by a surcharge on its product, or both? Or does it mean working with a different business model altogether?

My colleague Mohammad Yunus, for one, has been insistent about calling Teekampagne an example of "social entrepreneurship." We are a for-profit business and pay taxes, but if I ask the "cui bono?" question, I do see that our economic activity has quite a few beneficiaries. The list could include (but not necessarily be limited to) the following:

1. Our customers get an exquisite product (of unparalleled purity) at a low price.
2. The producers of our tea (owners as well as workers) get a decent price for their efforts.
3. We run a profitable company that employs people and gives work to other businesses.
4. Our Project SERVE has benefits for Darjeeling: we have planted 2 million seedlings so far, 70,000 last year alone, and such related projects as our model village Tinchulay or the Batasia Eco Garden produce long-term economic and educational results.
5. Our business model benefits the environment: using large packages reduces trash and cuts back on shopping trips; shortening the path from the producer to the consumer saves energy as well as money.
6. Resources have been made available to endow the "Stiftung Entrepreneurship" ("Faltin Foundation for Entrepreneurship") in Berlin. Its purpose is to show that important causes, addressed with creative ideas and artistic imagination, are at the root of entrepreneurial success, and to build bridges between business and social entrepreneurship.
7. Students and collaborators of mine have started successful companies of their own that apply the "campaign" principle of rational simplicity:

    a. Artefakt is a company that markets high-quality olive oil through the campaign method;
    b. Zait directs high-quality olive oil, wine, and other gourmet products directly from the producer to the consumer;
    c. Ratio Drink AG sells organic apple juice concentrate (add tap water and drink);
    d. Rapskernoel.Info offers cold-pressed organic canola oil;
    e. EBuero, which has 250 employees in Berlin alone, as well as branches in several European countries, offers low-cost virtual office support to anyone who needs a secretary;
    f. Teekampagne's latest venture is the already-mentioned CO_2 Campaign, the distribution (in large packets) of high-quality energy-saving light bulbs. (When our bulbs were featured – not advertised – on prime-time

German TV on July 16, 2008, our internet server collapsed under the inquiries that night).

The most lasting benefit is still evolving: my long-standing university workshop on generating and refining entrepreneurial ideas, in which I apply everything I have learned from my Teekampagne work, has encouraged a growing number of persons (not just students, but people of any age) to develop business ideas of their own. More importantly yet, it has sharpened my own concept of what I call "citizen entrepreneurship" or "entrepreneurship for all."

"Citizen Entrepreneurship": Self-Determination as a Philosophy of Life

"Everyone can be an entrepreneur," says Yunus. He has demonstrated in Bangladesh how even the poorest of the poor can take charge of their own life with micro-loans and a support system that helps them succeed. But is that experience universally applicable? In most countries, but certainly in the industrialized world, doesn't it require a lot of resources and expertise in business management to start a company?

Not necessarily.

First, let me point out that the customer can already be a co-entrepreneur. For instance, the Teekampagne customer orders a year's supply and provides storage (thus relieving us of this task). The Ratio Drink customer buys organic apple juice concentrate and adds water. In both cases, the customer understands the specific business concept and has a general understanding of how markets work. In both cases, the customer may become an ambassador for the company and the product. In both cases, the customer adds value and gets value in return. The customer thinks and works alongside the entrepreneur.

Secondly, what I teach in my workshops and what Teekampagne (along with its offspring) demonstrates is that an intelligent, sufficiently refined and developed idea is more important than the availability of resources or a complete understanding of business management. As to resources, experience shows that really good ideas do not necessarily require a huge amount of startup funding or, if they do, funding will follow and find them. With regard to business management, acquiring what some consider the "necessary" expertise can actually stand in the way of refining and implementing the business idea. Management expertise can be delegated and bought with relative ease; working through and refining concepts is something we need to do ourselves.

Thirdly and finally: Does it require genius to come up with a great business idea? Of course not. Idea generation and refinement can be learned and taught; in many instances, a successful business idea is the application of existing knowledge to a new field, the combination of existing ideas, or an improvement of something that already exists. What is required, however, is a focus on function and a willingness to break with convention. If Darjeeling is sold in 2 oz. packages, in stores, and in pretty wrapping, is that a convention or a necessity? Once I understand that such convention is not necessary for getting the tea to the consumer, I can begin to develop a different business model.

If entrepreneurs do not require huge capital or expertise or genius ideas to get going, what do they need? They need three things: appropriate methods and techniques to enhance initial ideas; perseverance; and faith in their ability to determine the course of their own lives.

The moral philosopher Adam Smith, known mostly for his book *The Wealth of Nations* (1776), already envisioned a form of "citizen entrepreneurship": the ability of individuals to participate in the marketplace as agents of their own fate. "Every man ... lives by exchanging, or becomes in some measure a merchant," says Smith, developing what his biographer Jerry Muller has termed "a vision of 'commercial humanism'" that is morally uplifting as well as practically empowering. To practice economic self-determination has long been recognized as a necessary (though not sufficient) condition for personal and political self-determination ("an empty sack cannot stand upright," we are told by Smith's contemporary and acquaintance, Benjamin Franklin). So considered, economic self-determination can become the basis of a life plan that conceives of a well-lived life as a multi-dimensional work of art. In our own day, the futurist Max Horx describes the ideal type that embodies this idea: "Our culture of individualism will produce a type of entrepreneur who will work for more than money, who wants to be good because she is ambitious – ambitious in a new, qualitative sense: he wants to create an individual life that is a work of art, as harmonious and exciting as possible." The citizen entrepreneur is that type: free to create, free to gain, and free to share.

Finally: have fun, in the sense of excitement, fulfillment, pride of accomplishment. Nothing is more exciting than to send a brainchild into the world and see it prosper. My students who started working on entrepreneurial projects did not just start new companies; they also re-fashioned themselves as human beings. They became more focused, more curious, and more communicative; their optimism and 'joie de vivre' was infectious; they even looked better. Were these changes the natural result of success? No – all of this happened before it was even clear whether their business idea would ever survive in the market. Was it because they were having fun? Yes, that too – but what really happened was that their life achieved a new direction and purpose; it gained meaning and perspective. Some are getting rich now; but that is not what makes their faces shine. They have become the entrepreneurs of their own lives.

References

Faltin, Guenter 2008
Kopf schlaegt Kapital, Hanser, München

Fleischmann, Fritz 2006
Entrepreneurship as emancipation: The history of an idea (lecture held in July 2006)
http://labor.entrepreneurship.de/tiki-index.php?page=Ressourcen

Horx, Matthias 2005
Wie wir leben werden. Unsere Zukunft beginnt jetzt. Campus Verlag, Frankfurt am Main

Kawasaki, Guy 2004
The Art of The Start. Penguin, New York

Yunus, Muhammad 2008
Die Armut besiegen. Hanser, München

Appendix

Declaration for All Life on Earth

Preamble

The earth is an evolving living entity. Every form of life on earth is an important part of this living entity. Accordingly, we, as individual human beings, must cultivate the awareness that we are all members of a global community of life and that we share a common mission and responsibility for the future of our planet.

Every one of us has a role to play in the evolution of our planet, and to achieve world peace each of us must live up to our responsibilities and obligations. Up to the present time, few people on earth have been fully satisfied with life. We have faced conflicts all over the world in competition for limited resources and land. This has had a devastating effect on the global environment.

As we enter the new millennium, more than anything else, the realization of world peace depends on an awakening of consciousness on the part of each individual member of the human race. Today, it is imperative that every human being bears the responsibility of building peace and harmony in his or her heart. We all have this common mission that we must fulfill. World peace will be achieved when every member of humanity becomes aware of this common mission— when we all join together for our common purpose.

Until now, in terms of power, wealth, fame, knowledge, technology and education, humanity has been divided between individuals, nations and organizations that have possession and those that do not. There have also been distinctions between the givers and the receivers, the helpers and the helped.

We hereby declare our commitment to transcend all these dualities and distinctions with a totally new concept, which will serve as our

157

foundation as we set out to build a peaceful world.

General Principles

In the new era, humanity shall advance to-ward a world of harmony, that is, a world in which every individual and every nation can freely express their individual qualities, while living in harmony with one another and with all life on earth. To realize this vision, we set forth the following guiding principles:

1. **Reverence for life**
   We shall create a world based on love and harmony in which all forms of life are respected.

2. **Respect for all differences**
   We shall create a world in which all different races, ethnic groups, religions, cultures, traditions and customs are respected. The world must be a place free from discrimination or confrontation, socially, physically and spiritually— a place where diversity is appreciated and enjoyed.

3. **Gratitude for and coexistence with all of nature**
   We shall create a world in which each person is aware that we are enabled to live through the blessings of nature, and lives in harmony with nature, showing gratitude for all animal, plant and other forms of life.

4. **Harmony between the spiritual and material**
   We shall create a world based on the harmonious balance of material and spiritualcivilization. We must break away from our overemphasis on the material to allow a healthy spirituality to blossom among humanity. We must build a world where not only material abundance but also spiritual riches are valued.

Practice

We shall put these principles into practice guided by the following:

As Individuals

We must move beyond an era in which authority and responsibility rest in nation states, ethnic groups and religions to one in which the individual is paramount. We envision an "Age of the Individual"— not in the sense of egoism, but an age in which every individual is ready to accept responsibility and to carry out his or her mission as an independent member of the human race.

Each of us shall carry out our greatest mission to bring love, harmony and gratitude into our own heart, and in so doing, bring harmony to the world at large.

In our specialized fields

We shall build a system of cooperation in which wisdom is gathered together to derive the most from technical knowledge, skills and ability in various fields, such as education, science, culture and the arts, as well as religion, philosophy, politics and economics.

As the young generation

In the 20th century, parents, teachers and society were the educators of children, and the children were always in the position of being taught. In the 21st century, adults shall learn from the wonderful qualities of children, such as their purity, innocence, radiance, wisdom and intuition, to inspire and uplift one another. The young generation shall play a leading role in the creation of peace for a bright future.

Authors

BABOS, PAOLA, is an Associate Expert with the United Nations in the Leadership and Capacity Development Unit of UN-OHRLLS. Focusing on the Least Developed Countries, Ms. Babos works with a range of stakeholders applying whole systems transformation and leadership development to achieve measurable and sustainable change in the domains of peace and development. Prior to joining the United Nations in New York City, Ms. Babos worked in the Balkans and other transition economies. She served in field positions in Serbia and Kosovo, focusing on post-conflict dialogue and reconciliation between Serb, Albanian and Roma communities in the aftermath of the Yugoslav wars. Ms. Babos holds a Bachelor of Science in Government and Economics from the London School of Economics and a Master's in International Relations from the University of Chicago. For more information, go to http://www.un.org/ohrlls

BOSCHEE, JERR, has been an advisor to social enterprises in the United States and elswhere for more than 30 years. To date he has been a keynoter or conducted workshops in 42 US States and 15 countries and has long been recognized as one of the founders of the social enterprise movement worldwide. Mr. Jerr is the Founder and Executive Director of The Institute for Social Entrepreneurs, one of the six Co-founders of the Social Enterprise Alliance, and the author or editor of five books in the field of social enterprise, including the award-winning publication, *Migrating from Innovation to Entrepreneurship: How Nonprofits are Moving toward Sustainability and Self-Sufficiency*. Mr. Jerr was named by *The NonProfit Times* to its nonprofit sector "Power & Influence Top 50" lists in 2004, 2005 and 2006. He also served from 2001 to 2004 as an advisor to England's Department of Trade and Industry Social Enterprise Unit. For more information, go to http://socialent.org

CECIL, CATHERINE, is Communications and Policy Advisor of Youth Star Cambodia. She is inspired by Youth Star's work to promote citizenship in Cambodia. With a long history of volunteering for many community organizations, Ms. Cecil is eager to see how strong citizenship values can help Cambodia moving forward. She has worked on many communication and policy projects for local and international organizations in Cambodia. Before she moved to Cambodia, Ms. Cecil worked as a legislative lawyer, focusing on healthcare and consumer issues. She also worked as the Director of Public Policy for an anti-hunger organization in Boston, MA in the USA. Ms. Cecil is a graduate of the University of Wisconsin and Northeastern University School of Law. For more information, go to http://www.youthstarcambodia.org

DRAYTON, BILL, Pioneer of the social entrepreneur movement, is the Chairman and CEO of Ashoka: Innovators for the Public. After graduating from Harvard, he received his M.A. at Oxford University and a J.D. from Yale Law School. He served in the Carter Administration as Assistant Administrator at the U.S. Environmental Protection Agency where he launched emissions trading (ultimately incorporated into the Kyoto protocol), among other reforms. Dr. Drayton has received numerous awards and honors. In 2005, he was selected one of America's Best Leaders by *US News & World Report* and Harvard's Center for Public Leadership, and was the recipient of the Yale Law School Award of Merit. In 2007, he has been awarded Duke University Center for the Advancement of Social Entrepreneurship's (CASE) Leadership in Social Entrepreneurship Award and the University of Pennsylvania Law School's 2007 Honorary Fellow Award. In 2009, he became a life Ballioll Honorary Fellow, Oxford University; and a distinguished honorary Doctor of Yale University was conferred upon him. Dr. Drayton is recipient of The Goi Peace Award 2007. For more information, go to http://www.ashoka.org

ELKINGTON, JOHN, is the Co-Founder of Volans Ventures, dedicated to supporting scalable entrepreneurial solutions to sustainability challenges. He is a leading authority on sustainable development and triple-bottom-line business strategy. Mr. Elkington was Co-Founder and a past Chairman (1996-2006) of SustainAbility; now he is the organization's chief entrepreneur. *Business Week* has described him "a dean of the corporate responsibility movement for three decades." *The Power of Unreasonable People* is his seventeenth book. He was Co-Author of *The Green Consumer Guide*, published in 1988, which sold around a million copies in twenty editions. His 1997 book, *Cannibals with*

Forks: The Triple Bottom Line of 21st Century Business, was a finalist for the Financial Times Global Business Book of the Year Award. He is a regular columnist for publications in Brazil, China, Japan, the United Kingdom, and the United States. Since 1974, Mr. Elkington has undertaken consultancy work for a variety of clients, including government agencies, companies and NGOs. He chairs the Environment Foundation and the advisory council of the Export Credits Guarantee Department. He is a member of the board of trustees of the Business & Human Rights Resource Center and the Council of the Royal Society of Arts, as well as a member of the advisory boards of Aflatoun, the Dow Jones Sustainability Indexes (Switzerland), Instituto Ethos (Brazil), Physic Ventures (USA), and Zouk Ventures (UK). Mr. Elkington has a BA in sociology and social psychology and a master's of philosophy in urban and regional planning. He has chaired or spoken at over 500 conferences and major events worldwide. In 1989, Mr. Elkington was elected to the UN Global 500 Roll of Honor for his "outstanding environmental achievements." For more information: http://www.johnelkington.com, http://www.volans.com

FALTIN, GUENTER, is a German Economist an Entrepreneur. He is Professor of Entrepreneurship at Freie Universität Berlin, and Founder of "Teekampagne," the largest mail order tea business in Germany. According to the Tea Board of India, "Teekampagne" has been the world's largest single importer of Darjeeling leaf tea since 1998. Noticing many years ago that tea was sold at schocklingly high prices, Professor Faltin looked for ways to challenge the traditional tea market. Thus, he created a new business model based on the principle of simplicity, which allows selling the world's best Darjeeling tea at very low prices and therewith making it affordable to many people. Professor Faltin teaches the principle of simplicity in business to students at Freie Universitaet Berlin and encourage them to become entrepreneurs themselves. He has published many papers and books on a culture of innovative entrepreneurship. His latest publication is entitled, *Kopf schlaegt Kapital. Die ganz andere Art, ein Unternehmen zu gruenden. Von der Lust, ein Entrepreneur zu sein* (2008). In 2007, Professor Faltin has received the "Vision Award for Entrepreneurship" at the Vision Summit taking place in Berlin in 2007. For more information, go to http://www.entrepreneurship.de

GAGNAIRE, KIRSTEN, has a broad background in developing strategy and conducting business planning for nonprofit, business and government clients. As Principal and Founder of Social Enterprise Group, LLC, Ms. Gagnaire specializes in assisting nonprofit and business clients in developing strategic plans, social enterprise business plans and building organizational capacity to achieve a more efficient and effective social enterprise. She is particularly adept at working with clients to turn challenges into opportunities and is skilled in bringing diverse stakeholders together to realize a common vision. Ms. Gagnaire was Administrator of Strategic Planning at Casey Family Programs. At Casey, she led the design, development and implementation of the foundation's most recent five-year plan, and served as an international consultant on organizational management and strategy issues. Ms. Gagnaire speaks at US and international conferences and universities on topics ranging from social emterprise to strategic plannning. She has a BA in Business Administration from Seattle University, USA. For more information, go to http://www.socialenterprisegroup.com

GALINSKY, LARA, is the Senior Vice President at Echoing Green. Her portfolio consists of the day-to-day management of Echoing Green, marketing and communications, evaluation, thought leadership, alliances, strategic planning, and internal capacity building. Most recently, Ms. Galinsky worked as the Director of National Programs at Do Something, Inc., working with over 20,000 educators to inspire 4 million young people to get involved in their communities and develop vital leadership skills. Before that, Ms. Galinsky launched the BRICK Award, which annually honors and funds the most outstanding community leaders under the age of thirty. She graduated Phi Beta Kappa from Wesleyan University and has completed executive programs at Columbia University Business School and Georgetown University's School of Public Policy. Ms. Galinsky serves as a board member for the Nonprofit Workforce Coalition, NYC Venture Philanthropy Fund, and the Fast Forward Fund, as well as the board Chair of StartingBloc. She recently graduated from Coro's Leadership New York program. For more information, go to http://www.echoinggreen.org

GUPTA, PARAG, is an Associate Director of the Schwab Foundation for Social Entrepreneurship and its Head for South Asia and Eastern Europe. His focuses include Philanthropy & Social Investing and Financial Empowerment. Mr. Gupta worked as a strategy consultant in the private, non-profit, and international development sectors. Previously, he was at the Bridgespan Group where he consulted to nonprofits and foundations.

Mr. Gupta has also independently advised social entrepreneurs in the United States, Central America, and South Asia on issues ranging from country industry growth to organizational expansion strategies to metric evaluation. He also founded a social enterprise dedicated to engaging Diaspora communities in building government-civil society partnerships and was recognized as one of the top 23 budding social entrepreneurs in 2006 by the Echoing Green Foundation. Mr. Gupta holds a Bachelor of Arts in Political Science from the University of Chicago with Honors. He also holds a Masters in Public Policy from the Kennedy School of Government at Harvard University. For more information, go to http://www.schwabfound.org

HARTIGAN, PAMELA, is Co-Founder of Volans Ventures, which aims to find, explore, advise on and build innovative scalable solutions to the great global divides that overshadow the future. Dr. Hartigan is the former Managing Director of the Schwab Foundation for Social Entrepreneurship, a Swiss-based organization founded by Klaus and Hilde Schwab in 1998, which focuses on building and supporting practioners whose efforts have achieved transformational change. She is a frequent lecturer on the topic of social entrepreneurship at graduate schools in the United States, Europe, and Asia. Throughout her career, Dr. Hartigan has held several leadership positions in multilateral health organizations and educational institutions as well in entrepreneurial nonprofits. She is on the board of a number of entrepreneurial start-ups and more established ventures. Of Ecuadorian origin, Dr. Hartigan received her BS in international economics from Georgetown University's School of Foreign Service, has an advanced degree in international economics from the Institut d'Études Européennes in Brussels, and earned a Master's in Education from American University in Washington D.C. Dr. Hartigan received her Ph.D. in human development psychology from Catholic University, Washington D.C. For more information, go to http://www.volans.com

HAWLEY, PAMELA, is Founder and CEO of UniversalGiving, a social entrepreneurship nonprofit organization whose vision is to "create a world where giving and volunteering is a natural part of everyday life." UniversalGiving has been featured in *CNNMoney.com*, *Time magazine*, *New York Times*, and *L.A. Times*. Ms. Hawley was Co-Founder of VolunteerMatch, a nonprofit organization, which has matched more than two million volunteers with nonprofits. She launched VolunteerMatch

Corporate (VMC), a customized version for corporations and their employee volunteer programs. More than 20 Fortune 500 companies became clients under her management (Charles Schwab, Coca-Cola, Dell, Duke Energy, Gap, Levi's, Merrill Lynch, Microsoft, Nike and Verizon) which contributed to 43% of the organization's sustainability. Ms. Hawley's community service began at the age of 12, and has extended into the international realm. She has worked and volunteered in microfinance in remote villages of India; crisis relief work in the El Salvador Earthquake; digital divide training in the Killing Fields of Cambodia; and sustainable farming in the countryside of Guatemala. Her studies include a political science degree cum laude at Duke University and scholarship in international communications masters at The Annenberg School of Communications, USC. For more information, go to http://www.universalgiving.org

PETIT, PATRICK U., is a Mediator (M.M.) and Start-Up Counsellor. Graduated in political science from the Munich School of Political Science, he is the Representative to the United Nations of the Goi Peace Foundation. In this capacity, Mr. Petit initiated and set up more than thirty peacemaking events worldwide in collaboration with regional and global Intergovernmental Organizations, as well as Parliaments and Parliamentary Assemblies. He organized two commemorative events on United Nations Day in 1999 and the consecutive year, while he has been the Representative to the United Nations of the World Peace Prayer Society in New York. Mr. Petit produced and moderated the cultural festivities of the Millennium Forum in 2000 at UN Headquarters. He is the initiator and editor of several publications: *Earth Capitalism* (2009), *The People's New Deal* (2009), *Earthrise* (2008) and *Wisdom 21: Shaping the Culture of Peace in a Multilateral World* (2005). Born in 1969 in France, Mr. Petit lives in Munich, Germany. For more information, go to http://www.goipeace.or.jp

RICKERT, ANDREAS, is Director at the Bertelsmann Stiftung and responsible for projects related to the future of civil society. Dr. Rickert currently leads the "Market Place for Social Investors" project at the Foundation. Prior to joining the Bertelmann Stiftung, Dr. Rickert worked as project manager with McKinsey and Company. He earned a Ph.D. from Stanford University, USA and has an MBA from Evian University, France. For more information, go to http://www.bertelsmann-stiftung.de

ROOF, NANCY, Ph.D., is the Founder and Editor-in-Chief of the integral global journal *Kosmos*, nominated for its excellence and spiritual coverage by the prestigious Utne Independent Press Awards. Kosmos brings leading edge ideas to United Nations Ambassadors, the UN Secretariat, NGOs and the international community of global citizens. Its unique mission is to create a sustainable, compassionate and emerging global civilization through individual, cultural, and systems transformation at all levels of body, mind, and spirit. Dr. Roof is Founding President of Kosmos Associates Inc. She co-founded the Values Caucus at the United Nations in 1994 with the help of Ambassador Somavia of Chile (now Director General of the UN International Labor Organization) and co-founded the Spiritual Caucus at the UN in 2000 for the purpose of bringing contemplation into UN deliberations. *Kosmos* is a founding partner of the worldwide initiative, ,Creating a New Civilization', launched by the Goi Peace Foundation in Tokyo, November 2005 with the Gorbachev Foundation, Club of Budapest, Club of Rome, Commission on Global Spirituality and Consciousness and World Wisdom Council. She is the first Media Ambassador invited to participate in the World Wisdom Council. Dr. Roof designed, implemented, and pioneered the first training programs in the former Yugoslavia on secondary traumatic stress in war zones. The program trained trainers of 78 organizations, including the United Nations, International Red Cross, governments, Doctors Without Borders, and local groups in three different locations. The program is now being used as a model in other War Zones. She published a widely distributed workbook for further self-training entitled *The Impact of War on Humanitarian Service Providers*. In the early 1970s she co-founded The Mountain School, to teach meditation and interior spiritual practices from a variety of religious traditions. Dr. Roof had a flourishing private practice in individual in-depth psychology based on the psychology she developed combining Western psychology and Eastern spiritual practices. For more information, go to http://www.kosmosjournal.org

SAIONJI, HIROO, is the President of The Goi Peace Foundation and its sister organization, The World Peace Prayer Society, a New York based Non-Governmental Organization associated with the Department of Public Information at the United Nations. Mr. Saionji is the great-grandson of Prince Kinmochi Saionji, who was twice Prime Minister of Japan during the Meiji Period. He is President of The Crescent, and a Member of the Alumni Association Board of Directors of Michigan State

University, where he earned a Master of Business Administration (MBA). Mr. Saionji is also a Member of the Board of Trustees of Gakushuin University. From 1974-1986, he was a business executive at the International Division of the Nippon Seiko Company. Mr. Saionji conceived the "Creating a New Civilization Initiative," which was launched by the Goi Peace Foundation, in collaboration with thirteen like-minded partner organizations on the occasion of the annual Goi Peace Forum in November 2005 in Tokyo. He travels extensively on speaking tours, and has led peace ceremonies in many countries as well as at the United Nations and other international organizations. Mr. Saionji and his wife, Masami Saionji, have received the Philosopher Shree Dnyaneshwara World Peace Prize, India in 2008. Both live in Tokyo and have three daughters. For more information, go to http://www.goipeace.or.jp and http://www.worldpeace.org

SCHOENING, MIRJAM, is Head and Senior Director of the Schwab Foundation for Social Entrepreneurship. She overseas the operations of the Foundation to ensure the selection of the highest quality of social entrepreneurs, and provides a unique platform for them to interact with decision leaders at the regional and industry level. Ms. Schoening is directly in charge of the Foundation's activities in Latin America and Europe. Mirjam joined the Schwab Foundation at its inception in August 2000. She graduated with a Master in Public Administration from the Harvard Kennedy School. Previously, she worked as a consultant at Bain & Company in Germany (1996-1998). In addition, she analyzed the social sector lending strategies in Southern Latin America for the World Bank, Washington, D.C. (1999) and reviewed investment decisions at Shell Scandinavia (1994-1995). She holds a Master in Business Administration from the University of St. Gallen, Switzerland, and studied at ESADE, Spain and the Stockholm School of Economics, Sweden. Her fields of expertise include social entrepreneurship, microfinance and social investing. Ms. Schoening's regional focus is Latin America, Europe and India. For more information, go to http://www.schwabfound.org

SHARMA, MONICA, M.D., is the Director, Leadership and Capacity Development, at the United Nations, OHRLLS in New York. Dr. Sharma is responsible for whole systems transformation and leadership development worldwide, with a focus on Least Developed Countries. She is pioneering generative and integral approaches leading to transformation on a global scale. She served in UNICEF in several global, regional and country positions that are meeting the needs of children worldwide. From 2000-2005 Dr. Sharma served as Director of HIV / AIDS for UNDP, generating 4.5 million people directly and influencing another 130 million people. In 2005 she and her team were honoured by UNDP for the best practice area. For more information, go to http:// www.un.org/ohrlls

SPIEGEL, PETER, is the Managing Director of GENISIS – Institute for Social Business and Impact Strategies in Berlin, Germany. He has been the Secretary-General of the Global Economic Forum (2005-2008) and of the Club of Budapest (2002-2005). Mr. Spiegel is a board member of the Committee for a Democratic UN, and Co-Initiator of the Global Marshall Plan Initiative. He also initiated and co-produced the annual Vision Summit in Berlin. Mr. Spiegel is (co-) author and editor of more than 20 publications; the most recent being, *Global Impact* (2009), *Muhammad Yunus – Banker der Armen* (2007), *Eine humane Weltwirtschaft* (2007), and *Kyoto Plus – So gelingt die Klimawende* (2006). He graduated in sociology at the University of Regensburg, Germany. Born in 1953 in Wuerzburg, Mr. Spiegel is married with three children and five grandchildren. For more information: http://www.peterspiegel.de, http://www. genisis-institute.org

TASAKA, HIROSHI, is the Founder and the President of Think Tank SophiaBank, a global network think tank that fosters social entrepreneurs to change paradigms of social systems. He is also the President of The Japan Social Entrepre-neur Forum (JSEF), a networking organization to promote collaborations among social entrepreneurs in Japan. Dr. Tasaka is a Professor at the Graduate School of Tama University in Tokyo, where he teaches the philosophy, vision, policy, strategy and skills of social entrepreneurs to create new social systems. He has worked as a member of the Global Agenda Council of the World Economic Forum since 2008. He has also worked as an advisor for various companies to support them to become social enterprises. Dr. Tasaka is a founding member of The Japan Research Institute. The Institute embraces the vision and strategy of "Industry Incubation," which aims to create new industries with private sector initiatives. As a member of the Board of Directors, he collaborated with over 700 companies to establish 20 consortia from 1990 to 2000. Born in 1951, Dr. Tasaka graduated from the University of Tokyo in 1974. In 1981, he earned a Ph.D. in nuclear engineering from Tokyo University. Dr. Tasaka is the author of more than 50 books, including,

To the Summit – Why Should You Embrace an Ideal in Your Heart; *The Five Laws to Foresee the Future*; *The Age of Living System Paradigm*; *The Gaia Perspective*; *What will Happen in the Knowledge Society*; and *Philosophy of Working*. For more information, go to http://www. sophiabank.co.jp or send email to tasaka@sophiabank.co.jp

YUNUS, MUHAMMAD, established the Grameen Bank in Bangladesh in 1983, fueled by the belief that credit is a fundamental human right. His objective was to help poor people escape from poverty by providing loans on terms suitable to them and by teaching them a few sound financial principles so they could help themselves. Since the mid-70s, the Grameen Bank has advanced to the forefront of a burgeoning world movement toward eradicating poverty through microlending. Replicas of the Grameen Bank model operate in more than 100 countries worldwide. From 1993 to 1995, Professor Yunus was a member of the International Advisory Group for the Fourth World Conference on Women, a post to which he was appointed by the UN Secretary General. He has served on the Global Commission of Women's Health, the Advisory Council for Sustainable Economic Development and the UN Expert Group on Women and Finance. Professor Yunus is the recipient of numerous international awards for his ideas and endeavors, including the Nikkei Asia Prize for Regional Growth (2004), Nihon Keizai Shimbun, Japan; Franklin D. Roosevelt Freedom Award (2006); and the Seoul Peace Prize (2006), Seoul Peace Prize Cultural Foundation, Seoul, Republic of Korea. On December 10, 2006 Professor Yunus received the Nobel Peace Prize. He was born in Dhaka, Bangladesh in 1940. For more information, go to http://www.muhammadyunus.org and http://www. grameen-info.org